By The Sea

by Sharyn Binam

T5-CVF-634

This book actually began in 1997 while I was drawing designs for The Sideload: Seashells. I must admit a great fondness for the beach and beach combing...and for seashells in particular. The colors, shapes and varieties of shells are simply unlimited: making them a perfect subject for painting. The layering of sideloaded acrylic permits a vast array of colors options. The seashore, like the desert, has an intensity and clarity of light. Colors can fade quickly in the sunshine but, I must admit to preferring a pastel palette. I hope that you find inspiration and a little fun while painting By the Sea.

There are three sections, with the majority comprised of the seashell designs. The 15 different shells are shown in the paint out on the center color pages. They are used in a variety of combinations for the shell designs. A tropical reef is featured in the whimsical designs for Beach Party (a set of plates, napkin rings, plate, utensil and napkin holders). Finally, there is just the beach...a truly simple and peaceful place...to watch the shore birds, build a sand castle or simply walk and look for treasures along the shore.

This is a special book for me, a mile stone of sorts...my twelfth book. I recall worrying that I might not be able to create enough for another book while I waited for the first to be published. I am not sure that writing a book has gotten easier but, I do not fear running out of ideas as I did 9 years ago. In fact, the next book is in the collecting and drawing stage...now I have more ideas than I have time to finish!

Happily Painting Always,

Sharyn Binam

Sharyn Binam, CDA,CCD

THREE WISHES
10841 E. Placita de Pascua
Tucson, AZ 85730

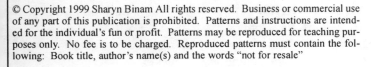

Would you like to meet people who share the same love of painting as you?
Become a member of The Society of Decorative Painters. For more information write:
The Society of Decorative Painters
393 N. McLean Blvd. • Wichita, • KS 67203-5968

Distributed by:
Essential Authors Services Ltd.
P.O. Box 22088 • St. Louis, MO • 63126
Phone: (314) 892-9222 • Fax: (314) 892-9607
Visit our web site at: http:\\www.easlpublications.com

Sources

Rectangular Box # 60154 and Cork Memo Board #61120 from:
CRAFTS AMERICANA GROUP
The Artist's Club
P.O. Box 8930
Vancouver, Washington 98668
Phone: (360)-260-8900
www.artistsclub.com

Utensil Holder #CE-074, Paper Plate Holder #CE-075, Napkin Holder #CE-067, Bucket #CE-076 and Lighthouse Birdhouse #CE-085:
THE CUTTING EDGE
P.O. Box 3000-402
Chino, California 91708
Phone: 909-464-0440
www.thecuttingedge-wood.com

Canvas Scrap Book/Memory Album #SBP11
DALEE BOOKBINDING
129 Clinton Place
Yonkers, New York 10701
Phone: 800-852-2665

French Portable Table #JB-503
J.B. WOOD PRODUCTS
1285 County Street
Attleboro, MA 02703
Phone: 800-859-4768
Fax: 508-222-9399

Lampshade Kit # 1913W:
KITI Division: Western Wireworks
300 N. Seminary Avenue
Woodstock, Illinois 60098
Phone: 800-435-8083

8 ½" Wood Plate #UPL0850:
MULTI-PLY
10 Edmund Avenue
Toronto, Ontario, Canada M4V 1H 3
Phone: 416-960-3034
Fax: 416-928-3441

Basket #600N:
PESKY BEAR
5059 Roszyk Hill Road
Machias, New York 14101
Phone/Fax: 716-942-3250

7" Lamp #17126 (Hardware Kit #7920), Plate Shelf #17135, 12" Corner Shelf # 7878 and Round Clock #23026 (Designer Hand Set #23092 and Clock #TQ700P) are from
Walnut Hollow whose products are available at leading craft departments throughout the country. For information on locating their products, contact them at :
1-800-950-5101
Or write to them at:
WALNUT HOLLOW
1409 State Road 23
Dodgeville, WI 53533-2112

Four Drawer Recipe Box with top storage #1454:
WAYNE'S WOODENWARE
1913 State Road 150
Neenah, Wisconsin 54956
Phone: 920-725-7986
Orders: 800-840-1497
Fax: 920-725-9386
e-mail: waynes@vbe.com

Expression Brushes and Arizona Wet Palettes:
THREE WISHES DECORATIVE ART
10841 E. Placita de Pascua
Tucson, Arizona 85730
Phone/Fax: 520-296-0309
e-mail:binam@theriver.com

Miscellaneous Supplies

BRUSHES: Robert Simmons Expression
E-51 18/0 Liner
E-51 10/0 Liner
E-51 #2 Liner
E-57 1/4" Angle Shader

E-57 3/8"Angle Shader
E-57 1/2" Angle Shader
E-57 5/8" Angle Shader
E-85 #4 Round

DELTA MEDIUMS:
All-Purpose Sealer
Color Float
Matte Exterior/Interior Varnish

ACCESSORIES:
Miscellaneous Supplies:
Lehigh #21 Cable Cord/Chalk Line (found in hardware stores or departments)
Delta Thick 'n Tacky Glue
A variety of Seashells, Starfish, Sand Dollars, etc.
Basket and/or Wreath

Almond Fashion Satin Spray (Wal-Mart)
Topiary Form and pot or bucket
Ivory Winter Cress (dried floral)
"Berry" spray in peach tones
Low Melt Glue Gun
Scissors and Wire Cutters

General Instructions

WOOD PREPARATION:

1. The quickest way to improve your painting is to improve your wood preparation. If, the wood is rough, sand well and fill any holes, cracks dents, etc. with a good wood filler. I like J.W., Etc.'s Wood Filler because it sands easily and dries quickly. And if, it dries out, just add water to the container and its usable again. Allow the filler to dry completely and then sand well. The Eversand sanding pads are great sanding tools.

2. Wood should always be sealed. Apply Delta Waterbased Sealer (#7005) with a large brush or sponge brush. When the sealer has thoroughly dried, sand lightly to knock down the grain.

3. Basecoat all of the wood pieces in BUTTERCREAM (#2523) with a dry sponge brush. Work paint into the sponge and scrub the paint into the wood following the grain. It is easier to control small amounts of paint and to eliminate drips and ridges that may occur with heavy applications of paint. Allow each coat of acrylic paint to cure dry 4 to 24 hours. Curing each coat of paint will leave a surface that is less easily damaged. The trim on all of the wood is RAW LINEN (#2546). The very neutral background colors should complement a variety of color schemes. However, any color from the palette may be used as a trim color.

4. After curing, sand lightly to knock down the grain and apply another coat of BUTTERCREAM. Again permit the surface to cure dry 4 to 24 hours. I generally do not sand after the final basecoat because I prefer a little tooth to the surface. Over-sanding can create a too slick finish. I find that my sideloads are easier to apply when there is a little tooth to the basecoat. For even more tooth, basecoat using a sponge roller.

TRANSFERRING THE DESIGN:

5. Place a piece of tracing paper over the design and tape in place with Drafting Tape. Use a .01 permanent ink pen or Technical pen and accurately trace the design.

6. Invest in a few good drawing tools such as a T-Square, a Circle Guide, French Curves, Oval Guide, flexible ruler and a compass. The foundation of a painting is the drawing. These tools will help you to transfer more quickly and accurately.

PAINTING THE DESIGN:

7. Tape the tracing of the design onto the surface. Use Super (blue) Chacopaper slipped under the tracing. Use the drawing tools to aid in transferring the design. Blue Chacopaper will also transfer onto glass, porcelain and glazed ceramic pieces. Most design have no area basecoats except on the underwater scenes for the Beach Party. I used a light wash of the first shading color to define the various elements since they are small and the patterns are complicated to apply. All shading, highlighting and tints are applied with a sideloaded angle brush.

DETAIL:

8. The details are applied with a sideloaded ¼-inch angle brush, a liner brush or a dip pen as indicated in the designs. Add the details after the first layer of the first shading color. For sideloaded details, tap in using the chisel edge of the brush. Tap from the outside edge of the shell into the center. The heel or back of the brush will deposit a little water that allows the color to bleed out slightly: which gives a more natural effect to the detail lines. For crisp lines use a new brush; for wider, less distinct lines use an older brush. If, the lines are too faint after shading and highlighting, they may be carefully re-applied where needed.

The sand was applied using a dip pen with a bowl pointed nib. The dip pen holds more paint than a stylus and makes smaller dots. It is also easier to control than a liner brush. Thin the paint with water to the consistency of ink. Make the mixtures in a paint pot strip. The paint stays fresh and dipping is easier.

9. Because my pieces were painted to be photographed, I did not use Pearl Finish (#2601) on the shells. The effect is perfect for seashells. Apply a single, even layer over the entire shell. It is very transparent so, none of the shading or highlighting is obscured. Pearl Finish gives a wonderful pearly glow. Do not apply to the Star Fish or Sea Horse as they have a rough texture.

FLOATING / SIDELOADING COLOR:

10. The correct balance between water and paint in sideloading is a difficult process to learn. If, there is not enough water the brush splits, the paint is streaked and the color is harsh. If, there is too much water, the color runs across the entire width of the brush leaving a waterline. Practice and experience eventually perfect the technique. However, Delta's wonderful Color Float really makes a big difference. Use just one drop per ounce of water in the brush basin used for sideloading. Color Float makes water wetter: making softer sideloads so much easier; there is no change in the drying time; and it does not weaken the bonding.

11. The most common mistakes that ruin a sideload start with trying to use too much paint and then not blending well enough on the palette. Truly, the most overlooked aspect is the work on the palette: which is probably the most important part in creating a good sideload. I cannot stress firmly enough: what you see on the palette is what you will see on the painting. All of the blending in the acrylic sideload is done on the palette. Proper blending is of equal importance to accurately placing the color on the painting.

12. I use the Arizona Wet Palette which Joanne and I have developed. It consists of lightly waxed paper (used by delis to wrap meat and cheese) called Kabnet Wax. I put a white paper towel inside and soak it in water. I place this on a sheet of man made chamois (the brand at K-Mart without the holes) to keep moisture in the palette all day. Smooth out any wrinkles and wipe off any puddles. There are two advantages to a wet palette: the paint stays usable for several hours and the wet surface helps to soften the color when sideloading. I use a heavy plastic tray to hold the wet palette and paper towels.

13. I sideload exclusively with Angle Shaders because the accuracy is unequaled. I cannot recommend an Angle Brush highly enough. I use 1/2", 3/8" and 1/4" as needed. My favorite is the Expression Series from Robert Simmons. The large handle is balanced and fits the hand causing less fatigue. The synthetic hair is exquisite. Sideloads are very soft and smooth because the hair is. And they last longer than any brush I have ever used. The larger handles also encourage a relaxed grip on the brush. If, the brush is held too tightly, the brush will not move freely.

14. To load the brush, first soak it thoroughly in water so, the hair under the ferrule is saturated. Brushes will come clean easier and the brush carries a reservoir of water. To remove the excess water, firmly drag the brush hairs over the lip of the Brush Basin to squeeze out the excess drop of water. I use my little finger to hold the Brush Basin steady. A hard sided brush basin is required for sideloading well. The basin is properly filled when the water is no deeper than the hairs of the brush. This leaves 3 areas of water: for cleaning the brush; rinsing the brush and sideloading the brush. Most important, it eliminates the need to wipe the water drops from the ferrule saving a lot of time and frustration.

15. Tip the brush with a small amount of paint. The more paint you use, the more difficult it is to control. The more pigment used, the more opaque the color will be. In transparent floated acrylics, transparency and accuracy are the principles of good technique.

The brush should be blended back and forth SLOWLY in a straight line using a great deal of pressure. Firmly pressing down while blending forces the paint toward the front of the brush. This allows more water to be used and controlled. Wimpy blending allows the paint to run across the width of the brush. The more blending, the softer the color becomes. Blend at least 8 to 10 times or until it becomes the color you need. What you see on the palette is what you will see on the painting.

The color should be blended into the brush about ½ to 2/3 of the length as well as the width of the brush. Proper blending allows the brush to carry more paint which can be placed with more control. The color should graduate across the width of the brush from dark to light to just water on the back of the brush.

The amount of pressure used when placing the color determines the amount of paint released by the brush. Without blending the paint well into the brush, most control over placing the color is lost. Under no circumstances should a ridge of paint develop at the top of your blending strip. The brush will also carry a ridge of paint. The color should graduate from dark to light leaving an even layer of paint on the palette.

I blend in a horizontal line and my sideloading partner, Joanne Hayman, blends vertically. Both are correct. One method will feel more comfortable then the other. You must be able to control the movement of the brush efficiently while blending. And you must be able to see exactly what you are doing whether blending or painting. If, you cannot see it, you cannot paint it! Position the palette and the surface in an easily reached and seen position. The length of the blending strip is best at about 1 inch.

16. Wash the brush out and re-load if, you see color across the width of the brush. Then blend in a new part of the palette. Color should never be visible on the back 1/3 of the brush. The color must fade from the darkest color on the tip, to just water on the back edge. If, a watermark appears, blend in a new part of the palette so, color is not picked up from a previous error. The wet palette permits you to blend in the same place each time without picking up specks of dried paint.

Color placement will be more accurate, easier and controlled with good palette work.

SHADING TECHNIQUE:

17. Sideloaded color is applied in thin, transparent layers. The first shading will probably appear blotchy. When a second float of that color is applied over the first dried layer, it will smooth out the color. This is the most important step in layering color. The first shading is the foundation for all subsequent colors. If, it is not done well, the rest of the painting suffers. Establish the first shadings on the design before applying the secondary shade color(s). Avoid applying so much color or so many layers that the transparency is lost (color becomes solid). If, you establish the first color well, it will discourage you from applying too much of the remaining colors. I feel that I paint best when I keep the colors transparent and not overwork the painting. The painting will look so much different with all of the shading, highlighting and tinting completed and too much fussing can ruin that final effect.

18. DO NOT OUTLINE! Making the shadings wide and narrow will more closely imitate natural shadows. To make wide areas of color, begin by filling a small area and then walk out the color: the paint tends to follow the water released by the brush as well as the motion of the brush. I use a small stroking motion (dab) to apply the paint. Dabbing releases small amounts of water on which the pigment floats. The color settles as the water dries. The paint will follow the brush so, move or stroke in the direction you wish the paint to go. Keep pulling the paint farther out until the desired width. I refer you to four of my previous books for more sideloading technique: The Sideload Book; The Sideload: Floral Techniques; The Sideload: Seashells and The Sideload: Rose Garden. The Sideload Book lessons are also available on The Sideload Video.

The best advice I can give is: think about where the color should be and analyze how best to place the color before you begin to paint. This will keep you from being tempted to touch up here and there: which only leads to smearing the color, pulling holes or creating a crusty ridge of color along the outside edge. Acrylic paint is just like Watercolors: they continue to work - all by themselves - until they are dry. Avoid painting next to an area that is wet as the paint can run. If, you paint transparently, a minor imperfection is easily fixed when that layer has dried. If, you wait, that minor imperfection may actually disappear on it own.

Use the brush flat on the surface: do not try to paint with just the tip of the brush. The back of the brush allows the color to graduate from dark to light. Do not be tempted to paint on the tip when you are in tight quarters. Because the color must be placed accurately with acrylics, we have to utilize a little geometry when painting. To make the sideload narrower, pull the back of the brush in toward the line to make the angle smaller. The widest mark that a brush will make is when it is perpendicular or 90 degrees to the line. When the angle between the brush and the line is smaller, the width of the sideload is smaller. Painting on the chisel or toe of the brush will leave texture marks.

If, the sideload needs to be wider, use a larger brush or walk out the color. To walk out the color, begin in the spot or area that will be the darkest (or lightest in the case of a highlight) and place the color accurately to fill the space. Move the brush about 1/8 inch out from this point and repeat the shape. Always begin and finish each stroke or pass into the outside lines. Each stroke of color should be placed before the color begins to change in the previous mark. I generally lift the brush at the end of each stroke so, that I begin and finish each stroke in the same direction. In repeating the same motion each time, eye/ hand coordination is improved. I use the pitty-pat motion to release a steady film of water. This film allows the paint to not only settle smoothly but, to flow freely and follow the movement of the brush.

To control the release of paint from the brush, increase or decrease the pressure used. Color will naturally be darker where the brush is first placed. To purposely leave more paint, apply more pressure to the brush. To leave less, use very little pressure. A light touch with the brush tends to create smoother color.

Shading and highlighting are used to create form and dimension in the painting. Form results not only in the contrast between light and dark but, also in the shape of the light and dark areas. Shading and highlighting must conform to the shape of the object. That is why merely outlining is so ineffectual: it does not create form nor does it conform to the shape of most objects. It makes two dimensions adequately but, not the third which creates volume. Use strokes that are shape following: if, an object is curved, show the curve in the color placement.

19. Allow each layer to completely dry before applying another layer of color. Try too soon and those holes are hard to repair. It is much easier to apply several layers of transparent color than one heavy layer. A mistake is easily removed, hidden or disguised when the color is transparent. It is time consuming and frustrating to try and repair errors made with a heavy sideload. I generally paint by applying one layer of the first shading to every area. I step away and analyze the overall effect as well as the form of each area or object. If, I have erred, it is easily repaired at this initial stage of the painting. The first shading is the foundation supporting the painting. If, it is not correct, subsequent layers will only compound the error (and I will find myself fussing too much).

The first shading divides and separates object and areas; establishes the shape and form; and thus creates depth and dimension. The color should be smooth and the edges always crisp and clean. Correct any errors in the first layer of color with the second transparent layer. The areas marked with dots [:::::] on the shading diagrams indicate the placement for the first shading color.

Shading colors are generally applied using the basic strokes for Triangles, Pivots, Crescents and Tornadoes. The shading on the basket (Basket of Shells) is more of an edge-to-edge shading but, maintain the curved appearance of the woven reeds. On many of the shells, the first shading defines indented or raised sections. Keep the color placement as accurate as possible to establish those features.

20. Secondary shade colors are applied in the same shapes but, in smaller areas over the first shading. Sometimes, a second shading color is not used over every area with a first shading color. Remember we are creating form and the variety of light and dark help create that illusion. Second shadings are indicated with cross-hatching on the shading placement diagram.

The second shading continues to separate objects and areas. It reinforces the shapes of objects as well as place them within the planes of the painting. Creating the front, middle and back planes within a painting visually creates the volume of objects. Color manipulation is our principle method of creating dimension. Basically: dark, dull and cool colors visually recede in the painting; light, bright and warm colors come forward.

The third shading color, or Core Dark, further accentuates the dimension. They are shown with solid color inking on the second shading diagram. You will notice that the core darks are much smaller than the first two colors placed and are usually triangular in shape. Maintain the transparency of these very dark colors.

21. Highlights on the shells are built up in the same way as shadings: use two layers of the low light, LIGHT IVORY, and then one layer of the highlight, WHITE. Because the shells have a glossy appearance, White makes the shine on shell surfaces. To create the pearly look, apply a layer of PEARL FINISH over the entire shell when completed. Some of the shells use WESTERN SUNSET YELLOW as the low light and then LIGHT IVORY for the highlight for variety. The Background color BUTTERCREAM works as part of the highlighting making it easier to control the whites: eliminating the chalky look. Highlights are indicated with [xxXxx] on the diagrams.

Highlights are usually Pivots when found along an edge; Circular or oval when they are placed inside an area; or as Tornado shapes to lift an area of the shell. The tornado shapes may be alternated with shaded areas to create ridging or ripples. Tornadoes have the darkest or lightest color along the center line with the color fading to either side of that center line.

22. Tints are applied using very light color so, they are not overwhelming. Again layering allows you to judge the color and make adjustments easily. The tint colors are placed inside the shell opening. Tints are indicated with [ooOoo]. If, tint colors are layered, gradually reduced the area covered by the additional colors.

Tints are usually applied as Pivots. The center of the pivot may be quite wide and that requires the color be walked out in the center of the pivot . All of the tints are warm accents found in the shell openings or along edges.

FABRIC PAINTING:

23. If, you wish to paint any of the designs on canvas surfaces such as tote bags, use Delta Textile Medium. I put the Textile Medium in a small plastic container and use the medium to dress the brush rather than water. Then, as I load the paint into the brush, the Textile Medium is blended into the paint. I basecoat each area, then sideload the shading and highlight colors into the damp basecoat.

24 To paint on Creations in Canvas, first apply a coat of Matte Varnish to the surface. Sand smooth when dry and apply a second layer of varnish. This will make the surface easier to clean up. By the Sea was painted on a Memory/Scrapbook. Many of the designs would be great for other Creations in Canvas pieces. No Textile Medium is needed for Creations in Canvas.

FINISHING:

25. To protect all of your hard work, spend a little extra time to finish well. I use Delta Matte Exterior/Interior Varnish. It dries quickly, brush marks settle out quite well and it does not yellow. Use a large, soft brush to apply several coats. A light polishing with 0000 Steel Wool after the varnish is dry will remove any shine. I try to use a minimum of 4 to 6 coats of varnish. The varnish dries very hard providing excellent protection.

26. If, you prefer to use a spray finish, try Delta Acrylic Satin or Matte Finish Spray. Spray outside and allow to dry before bringing the piece inside. Use several very light coats to seal before applying heavier applications.

29. For exterior use, I use the Matte or Satin Exterior / Interior Varnish which is a polyurethane. Use at least 4 coats of varnish. You may steel wool to knock down a little of the shine. Apply a paste wax to the entire surface. This will fill any small cracks and therefore prevent peeling. Once a year, wash with a mixture of water and ammonia to remove the wax. Apply a new coat of paste wax.

Beach Scenes Palette

Delta Ceramcoat

2025	Burnt Umber
2055	Autumn Brown
2098	Tomato Spice
2118	Lichen Grey
2401	Light Ivory
2402	Sandstone
2416	Liberty Blue
2425	Territorial Beige

2430	Rosetta Pink
2435	Trail Tan
2436	Charcoal
2440	Bridgeport Grey
2445	Green Sea
2447	Village Green
2454	Western Sunset Yellow
2466	Dunes Beige
2468	Ice Storm Violet

2473	Pale Mint Green
2488	Mudstone
2505	White
2516	Calypso Orange
2523	Buttercream
2527	Dark Burnt Umber
2532	Light Sage
2546	Raw Linen
2548	Purple Smoke

Beach Scenes Shading Chart

AREA	SHADING	HIGHLIGHT	ACCENT	DETAILS
Sand	1: Raw Linen 2: Sandstone 3: Trail	Light Ivory		Grains: Sandstone OR Trail
Sky	1: Light Sage			
Sea	1: Pale Mint Green 2: Pale Mint + Village Green			
Beach Grass	1: Village Green 2: Village + Green Sea 3: Green Sea	Western Sunset	Dark Burnt Umber	
Rocks	1: Buttercream + Lichen Grey 2: Lichen Grey	1: Ice Storm 2: White		
Pail and Shovel	1: Ice Storm 2: Ice Storm + Bridgeport 3: Purple Smoke + Bridgeport	1: Light Ivory		
Flag	1: Western Sunset 2: Rosetta	Light Ivory		Strings: Bridgeport
Sanderlings	1: Buttercream + Lichen Grey 2: Lichen Grey 3: Mudstone	1: Light Ivory 2: White		Tummy Dots Raw Linen
Sea Gulls	1: Soft Grey 2: Bridgeport 3: Charcoal	1: Light Ivory 2: White		Beak & Legs:Custard Shade:Calypso
Starfish	1: Western Sunset 2: Territorial Beige	1: Light Ivory		Dots:WesternSunset
Sea Snail	1: Ice Storm 2: Ice Storm +Purple Smoke	1: White	Dark Umber	Lines: Ice Storm + Purple Smoke
Scallop	1: Raw Linen 2: Sandstone 3: Lichen Grey	1: Light Ivory 2: White	Rosetta	Line: Sandstone
Auger	1: Trail 2: Territorial Beige 3: Dark Umber	1: Light Ivory	Rosetta	Line: Trail
Sand Dollar	1: Ice Storm 2: Lichen Grey	1: Light Ivory 2: White		Sandstone
Nautilus	1: Raw Linen 2: Sandstone 3: Lichen Grey	1: Light Ivory 2: White	Autumn Brown	Stripes: Autumn Brown

Shore Patrol

At the Beach...
wish you were here!

10

By The Sea

Shore Bird Decoys

Directions for painting the decoys is found on page 13

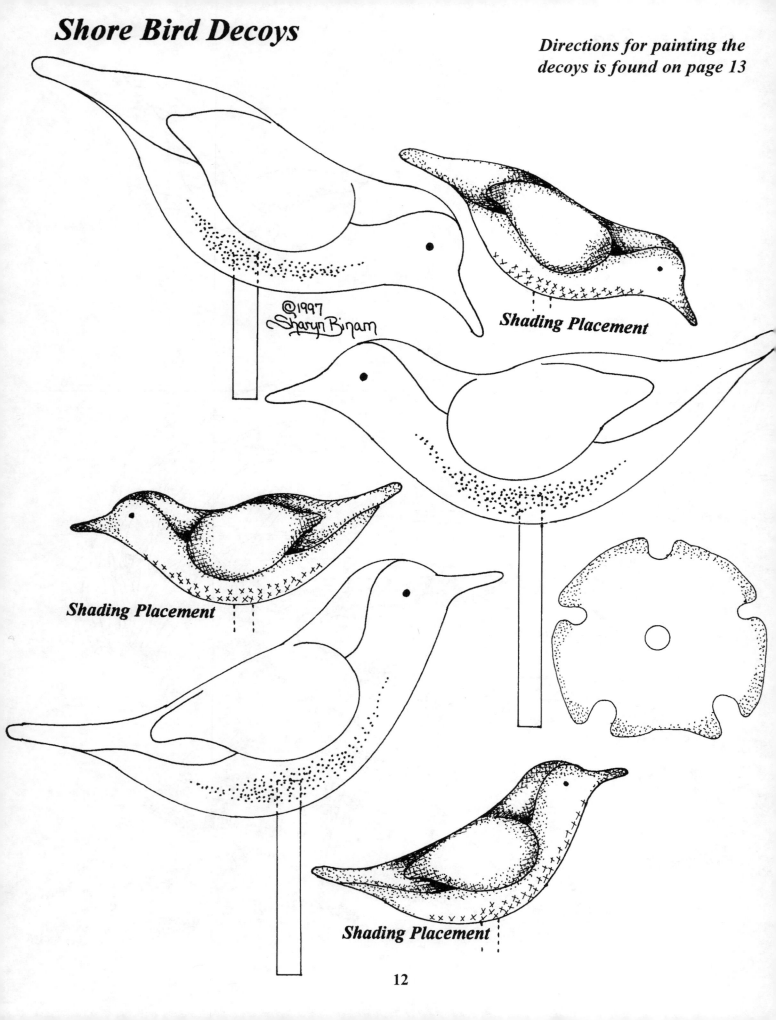

@1997
Sharyn Binam

Shading Placement

Shading Placement

Shading Placement

Painting the Lighthouse

The instructions for painting all of the beach scenes are included with the Lighthouse as the various elements are similar for all. Again, all of the surface basecoats are Buttercream with trim in Raw Linen. The top of the Lighthouse is edged in Lichen Grey around the top section. Refer to the shading placement diagrams while placing color. The smaller parts of the design are shown enlarged on the detail and shading diagrams.

The Siding:
Transfer the design with Superchaco paper and stylus using a ruler for all straight lines and a circle guide for the round windows. Shade under each board and around the other parts of the design with Raw Linen. Designs for 3 sides are provided, the fourth side is just siding. Extend the lines across the back with a ruler and white chalk pencil or soapstone. Once all of the siding has been shaded, apply the first shade color to the remaining areas to set the design. Clean up edges, if necessary. Deepen the shading under the boards and design with Sandstone. Darken under the top and the various designs with Lichen Grey. Highlight the edge of the boards with White.

The Door:
Shade around the crossed boards and the door frame with a mix of equal parts of Buttercream and Lichen Grey. Deepen the shading with Lichen Grey. If more contrast is preferred, deepen the shading with a mix of Lichen Grey and Dark Burnt Umber. Highlight the edges of the frame with White.

The Doorknob and Hinges:
Shade with Bridgeport Grey along the lower edge of the hinges and the knob. Deepen the shading with a mix of Bridgeport and Charcoal. Highlight the tops with White. The nails on the hinges are dots of Soft Grey.

The Windows:
Shade around the round windows while painting the siding. Shade inside the window openings with Raw Linen. Deepen the shading with Sandstone. Darken with a transparent sideload of Territorial Beige. Highlight the window frame with White.

The Flag:
Apply the colors of the Flag with a wash of color: red stripes are Tomato Spice; white stripes are White and the blue field is Liberty Blue. Shade the edges of the red stripes and the blue area with the wash color. Shade under the entire fold and along the edges with Bridgeport Grey. Deepen the

shading with a mix of Bridgeport and Liberty Blue. Highlight the flag with White. Ties are Bridgeport Grey.

The Flag Pole and Lantern:
Shade both with Bridgeport Grey. Refer to the lantern enlargement for color placement. Deepen the shading with a mix of Bridgeport Grey and Charcoal. For more contrast on the lantern: darken further with Charcoal. Highlight through the center on both with White. The glass in the lantern is accented with white on the outside edge and then down the center with the rest of the lantern. The hanger for the lantern is shaded with Territorial Beige. The nail is Soft Grey.

The Life Ring:
Shade the inside and outside edges with Raw Linen. Deepen the shading with a mix of Raw Linen and Lichen Grey. The rope is lined using 's' marks of Lichen Grey (18/0 Liner) and then shading is placed between the wrappings with Dark Burnt Umber (use very light color).

The Sea Gulls:
Shade under the wings and head and across the back with Soft Grey using the shading diagram as a guide. Deepen the shading with Bridgeport Grey. Darken further with Charcoal using fairly light color. Highlight the wing edge and the chin with White. Tap in the dark wing and tail feathers with a mix of Bridgeport and Charcoal sideloaded on a ¼" Angle. The legs and beak are washed with Custard and then shaded with Calypso Orange. The eye is a dot of Charcoal.

The Sanderlings (and Decoys):
Shade under the wings and across the back, head and beak with a mix of Buttercream and Lichen Grey using the shading diagram as a guide. Deepen the shading with Lichen Grey. Darken further with Dark Burnt Umber. Highlight the tummy and the wing with Light Ivory and then brighten the highlight on the tummy with White. Dots along the tummy are Lichen Grey (or Sandstone). For larger birds, shade under the wing and top with Sandstone. The eye is a dot of Dark Burnt Umber.

The Pelican:
Shade the entire Pelican with Raw Linen using the shading diagram as a guide. Deepen the shading on the body and wing with Lichen Grey. Tap in the wing and tail feathers with a sideloaded ¼" Angle using Bridgeport Grey. Deepen the shading with a

mix of Lichen Grey and Dark Burnt Umber. Shade the feet and inside the bill with Western Sunset Yellow. Deepen the shading with Territorial Beige. Shade the outside of the bill with Lichen Grey and then deepen the shading with Charcoal. The head and neck are shaded with Burnt Umber. The top of the head is highlighted down into the face with White. The face next to the bill is tinted with Calypso Orange. The eye is a dot of Charcoal.

The Pail (and Shovel):
Shade with Violet Ice along the edges and under the rim of the bucket and the handle of the shovel. Deepen the shading with Bridgeport Grey (add a touch of Violet Ice to make the color transition easier). Deepen the shading with a mix of Bridgeport and Charcoal. Highlight the center of the pail and the right side of the shovel with White.

The Barrel:
Shade both edges of the slats, under the barrel rings and the curved ends of the top with Trail Tan. Line the slats with Lichen Grey to create the wood grain. Shade the rings with Bridgeport Grey. The shading may be deepened further with a mix of Bridgeport and Charcoal. Deepen the shading on the barrel along the outside edges, under the rings and the top with Territorial Beige. Darken the shading further with Burnt Umber. Highlight the center of the barrel with Light Ivory. The rings may be highlighted with White.

The Anchor:
Shade the edges with Soft Grey. Deepen the shading with Bridgeport Grey. Darken further with a mix of Bridgeport and Charcoal. Highlight the points with White. Line the rope with Lichen Grey using 's' marks with an 18/0 Liner. Shade under the rope with Charcoal on the anchor and with Lichen Grey on the building.

The Rowboat and Oars:
Shade the boards in the rowboat and the edges of the oars with Trail Tan. Tap in the wood grain with Lichen Grey sideloaded on a ¼" Angle. Deepen the shading with Territorial Beige. Darken further along the bottom edge of the boat and the oars and under the Pelican with Dark Burnt Umber.

The Nautilus:
Shade the entire shell with Raw Linen and then deepen the shading with Lichen Grey. Line the stripes with Autumn Brown. Shade the stripes and the inside curve of the shell with Autumn Brown. Highlight the center curve of the shell with White.

The Scallop:
Line the segments of the shell with Raw Linen. Shade the top and bottom with Raw Linen. Deepen the shading with Sandstone. Darken the shading at the bottom curve with Lichen Grey. Tint the shell with two areas of Rosetta. Highlight between the tinted areas with White.

The Sea Snail:
Line the curves of the shell and then shade with Ice Storm. Deepen the shading with a mix of Ice Storm and Purple Smoke. Using an 18/0 Liner, dot in the detail with this color around the shell. Tint inside the opening with Dark Burnt Umber. Highlight along the opening and the center of the curves with White.

The Augur Shell:
Shade the top and bottom curve of each segment with Raw Linen and pull the color in a line between the segments. Align the brush with the segments to define the center shading under each segment. Deepen the shading with Territorial Beige. Darken further with Dark Burnt Umber along the bottom edge. Tint the inside opening with Rosetta. Highlight through the center of the shell with Light Ivory.

The Sand Dollar:
Dot all of the details inside the Sand Dollar with Raw Linen (or with Lichen Grey) using an 18/0 Liner. Shade the outside edge with Ice Storm. Deepen the shading along the bottom edge with Lichen Grey. Highlight the center with White.

The Clam Shell:
Shade along the segments with Western Sunset Yellow (make small tornado shapes into each segment line from the outside edge). Deepen the shading with Territorial Beige. Line or tap in the curved lines across the shell with Rosetta. Highlight the center of the shell with White.

The Star Fish:
Shade the end and bottom edge of each arm with Western Sunset Yellow. Dots in the center of each arm are Territorial Beige made with an 18/0 Liner. Deepen the shading with Territorial Beige. Highlight the center line of each arm with White.

The Beach Sand:
Thin Sandstone with water to the consistency of ink. Use a dip pen to make the grains of sand as indicated on the detail diagrams. Allow the dots to dry thoroughly. Shade under the objects on the beach with Sandstone. Deepen the shading with Trail. The dunes may be highlighted with Light Ivory on the light side of each dune.

The Beach Rocks:

Tap in a random wash of the mix of Buttercream and Lichen Grey (or Bridgeport Grey). Shade the lower edge of the rocks with Lichen Grey. Tap in a random highlight of Ice Storm or White using the side of side-loaded brush. For more contrast, randomly dab in Dark Burnt Umber along the bottom edge of the rocks.

The Beach Grass:

Apply a wash of Village Green over the blades with a #1 or #2 Liner. Shade along one side to separate the blades with a mix of Village Green and Green Sea. Deepen the shading with Green Sea. Highlight the turns with Western Sunset. Shade the clump along the bottom with a light sideload of Dark Burnt Umber.

The Sky:

Shade the corners and behind the sand with Light Sage for the Sky. This muted blue-green appears blue against the Buttercream background.

The Sea:

On the design "By the Sea", the water separates the beach and sky. Shade the back and front edges of the sea with Pale Mint Green. Deepen the shading near the shore with a mix of Pale Mint Green and Village Green. Tap in horizontal lines with this same mixture.

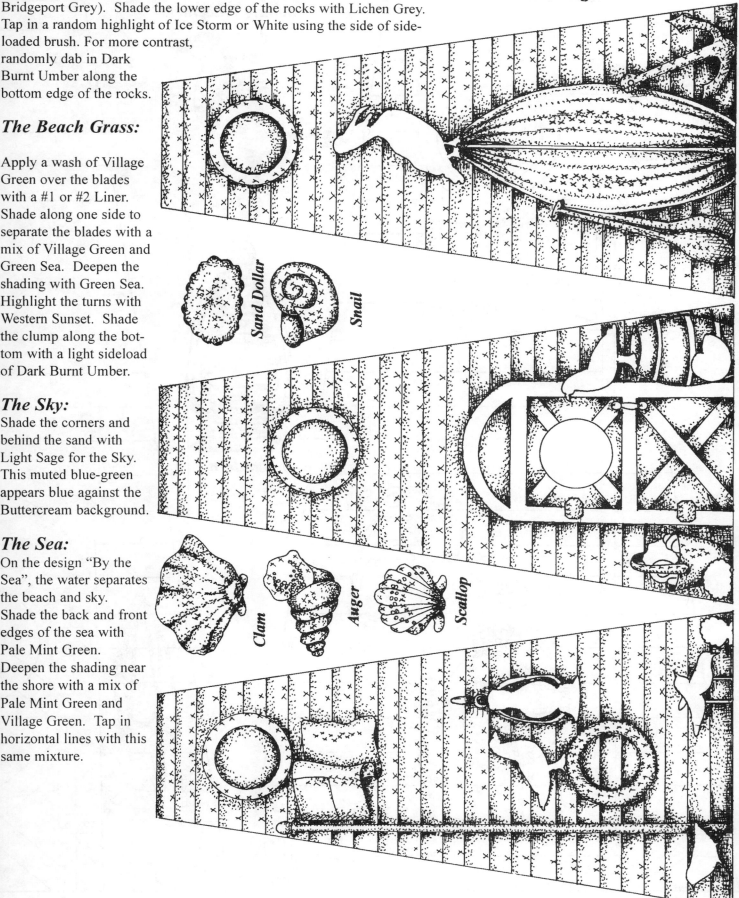

Sand Dollar

Snail

Clam

Auger

Scallop

15

The Lighthouse

Sanderling

Shading Placement

Sea Gull

Lantern

©1999
Sharyn Binam

16

Shading Placement

Pelican

Nautilus

17

Beach Party Palette

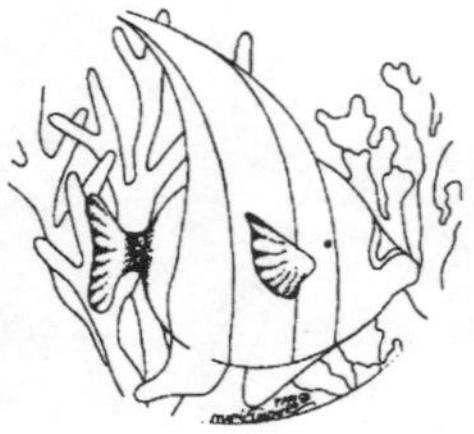

Delta Ceramcoat

2025	Burnt Umber	2448	Custard	2532	Light Sage
2050	Mocha Brown	2454	Western Sunset Yellow	2546	Raw Linen
2115	Blue Spruce	2459	Crocus Yellow	2548	Purple Smoke
2118	Lichen Grey	2466	Dunes Beige	2550	Oasis Green
2401	Light Ivory	2468	Ice Storm Violet	2557	Violet Ice
2402	Sandstone	2472	Santa's Flesh		
2424	Bambi Brown	2494	Heritage Green		
2425	Territorial Beige	2496	Santa Fe Rose		
2430	Rosetta Pink	2505	White		
2436	Charcoal	2506	Black``		
2440	Bridgeport Grey	2516	Calypso Orange		
2447	Village Green	2523	Buttercream		
		2527	Dark Burnt Umber		

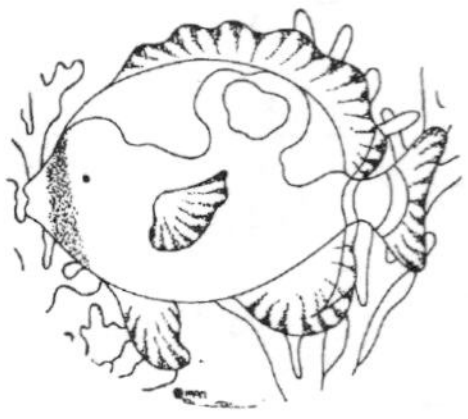

The Tropical Fish:

The **tropical fish plates and napkin rings** are basecoated with Buttercream. Trim the rim of the plates with a mix of Oasis Green and Buttercream. Basecoat the back and edge with Oasis Green. Shade from the edge onto the trim with Oasis Green. Shade from the trim into the center with the mix of Oasis and Buttercream. The background design for all of the fish is Soft Coral and Blue Coral.

The napkin rings are based with the Oasis and Buttercream mix. I used a small piece of ¼" dowel and drilled holes about 1/8" deep in the napkin ring and the cutout and then glued (and clamped) the pieces. I was lucky to find napkins just slightly darker than Oasis Green. I added inexpensive plastic handled silverware a shade darker than Oasis to the picnic set.

Beach Party Shading Chart

AREA	SHADING	HIGHLIGHT	ACCENT	DETAILS
Moorish Idol	1: Sandstone 2: SS + Bridgeport 3: Bridgeport Grey	1: Light Ivory 2: White	1: Custard 2: Crocus 3: Heritage + (Bridgeport)	Bridgeport
Stripe *Tail*	1: Bridgeport 2: Charcoal 3: Black		1: Custard 2: Calypso 3: Santa Fe Rose 4: Blue Spruce	
Butterfly Fish #1	1: Sandstone 2: Sandstone +Bridgeport 3: Bridgeport	1: Light Ivory 2: White	1: Heritage Green	
Spots *Fins*	1: Custard 2: Crocus 3: Calypso	1: Light Ivory 2: White	1: Santa Fe Rose 2: Bridgeport	Stripes: Charcoal
Face	1: Bridgeport 2: Blue Spruce			
Butterfly Fish #2	1: Custard 2: Custard + Crocus 3: Mocha Brown	1: Light Ivory 2: White	1: Heritage Green	Fins: Bridgeport Stripes: Mocha
Eye Spot	1: Bridgeport			
Fins:	1: Custard 2: Mocha Brown		1: Santa Fe Rose	Fins: Bridgeport
Queen Angel Fish	1: Custard 2: Custard + Crocus 3: Heritage Green	1: Light Ivory 2: White	1: Santa Fe 2: Blue Spruce	Scales: Oasis Green

Rock Beauty Angel Fish	1: Custard 2: Crocus 3: Calypso	1: Light Ivory 2: White	1: Heritage 2: Bridgeport	Tail Stripe: Light Sage Fins: Bridgeport Scales: Oasis
Clown Fish	1: Western Sunset 2: Calypso 3: Santa Fe Rose	1: Light Ivory 2: White		Stripes: Light Ivory
Anemone Fish	1: Custard 2: Crocus 3: Rosetta	1: Light Ivory 2: White	1: Heritage	Stripes: Light Ivory
Sea Horse	1: Dunes Beige 2: Bambi Brown 3: Burnt Umber	1: Light Ivory 2: White	Lichen Grey	Centerline: Dunes +Bambi
Sea Turtle	1: Light Sage 2: Oasis Green 3: Bambi + Heritage	1: Light Ivory	1: Bambi	Toes: Oasis Green
Crab	1: Dunes Beige 2: Rosetta 3: Santa Fe Rose	1: Custard		Mouth: line in Bridgeport
Star Fish	1: Western Sunset 2: Territorial Beige 3: Burnt Umber	1: Light Ivory		Dots: T. Beige
Sand Dollar	1: Ice Storm 2: Lichen Grey	1: White		Raw Linen
Scallop	1: Raw Linen 2: Sandstone 3: Lichen Grey	1: Light Ivory 2: White	1: Rosetta	Line: Sandstone
Sea Snail	1: Ice Storm 2: Ice + Purple Smoke	1: White	1: Dark Umber	Lines: Ice Storm + P. Smoke
Auger Shell	1: Raw Linen 2: Bambi Brown 3: Dark Umber	1: White	1: Rosetta	
Soft Coral	1: Village Green 2: Village + Heritage 3: Heritage Green	1: Custard		
Blue Coral	1: Light Sage 2: Sage + Heritage 3: Mix + P. Smoke	1: Violet Ice		
Sea Fan	1: Violet Ice 2: Light Sage + Oasis 3: Oasis Green	1: Ice Storm		
Tube Sponge	1: Violet Ice 2: V. Ice + P.Smoke 3: Purple Smoke	1: White	1: Ice Storm	Dots: Purple Smoke
Anemone	1: Oasis Green 2: Oasis Green + Heritage Green			
Sea Grass	1: Village Green 2: Village + G. Sea 3: Green Sea			
Rocks	1: Bridgeport 2: Lichen Grey 3: Dark Burnt Umber	1: Light Ivory		
Sand	1: Sandstone 2: Trail 3: Territorial Beige			Grains: Sandstone

Beach Party:
Moorish Idol

Moorish Idol Directions

The body of the Moorish Idol is shaded with Sandstone between the two dark stripes and along the narrow section of the tail. Deepen the shading with a mix of Sandstone and Bridgeport Grey. Darken further with Bridgeport. Apply a wash of Bridgeport over the stripes and the small stripe on the face. Shade the outside edges of the stripes with Charcoal and then deepen the shading further with Black. Tint the body area on both sides of the back stripe with Custard. Deepen the tint with Crocus. Accent the face and tail area with Blue Spruce (or Heritage Green). Tap in the fin with a ¼" Angle using a mix of Heritage Green and Bridgeport Grey. Tint the face patch (surrounded by the small stripe) and the fin with Custard. Deepen the tinting with Calypso Orange. Darken with Santa Fe Rose. Highlight the center line of the fish with Light Ivory. Brighten the highlight with White. The eye is a dot of Black.

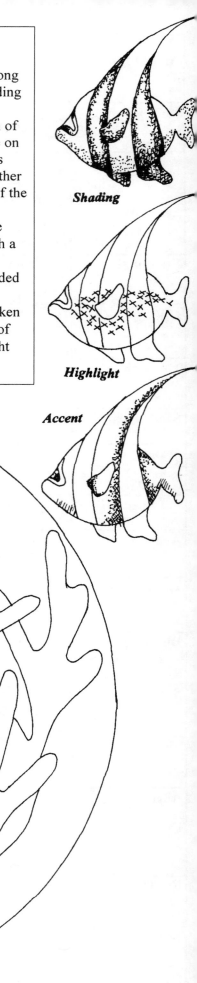

Shading

Highlight

Accent

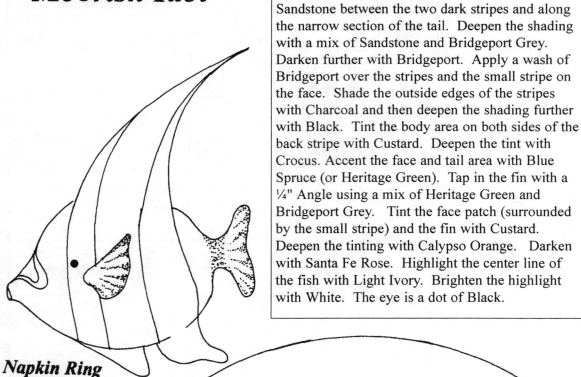

Napkin Ring Cutout

©1997
Sharyn Binam

20

Beach Party:
Butterfly Fish #1

Butterfly Fish #1 directions:

Shade the lower body area with Sandstone. Deepen the shading with a mix of Sandstone and Bridgeport. Darken further with Bridgeport Grey. Tap in the fins and tail with a ¼" Angle with Bridgeport Grey. Tint the top spots, the fins and a stripe on the tail with Custard. Deepen the tinting with Crocus and then intensify further with Calypso Orange. Accent the fins with Santa Fe Rose on the front of the fins and Heritage Green on the back. Sideload a wide stripe over the face (using a back to back sideload) of Bridgeport. Shade the bottom edge of the center spot with Bridgeport. Deepen the coloring with Blue Spruce. The back edge of the fins has a stripe of Charcoal. Shade along the back edge of the stripe with Black. Highlight the center of the fish and the fins with Light Ivory. Brighten with White. The eye is a dot of Black.

Napkin Ring Cutout

Shading

Highlight

Accent

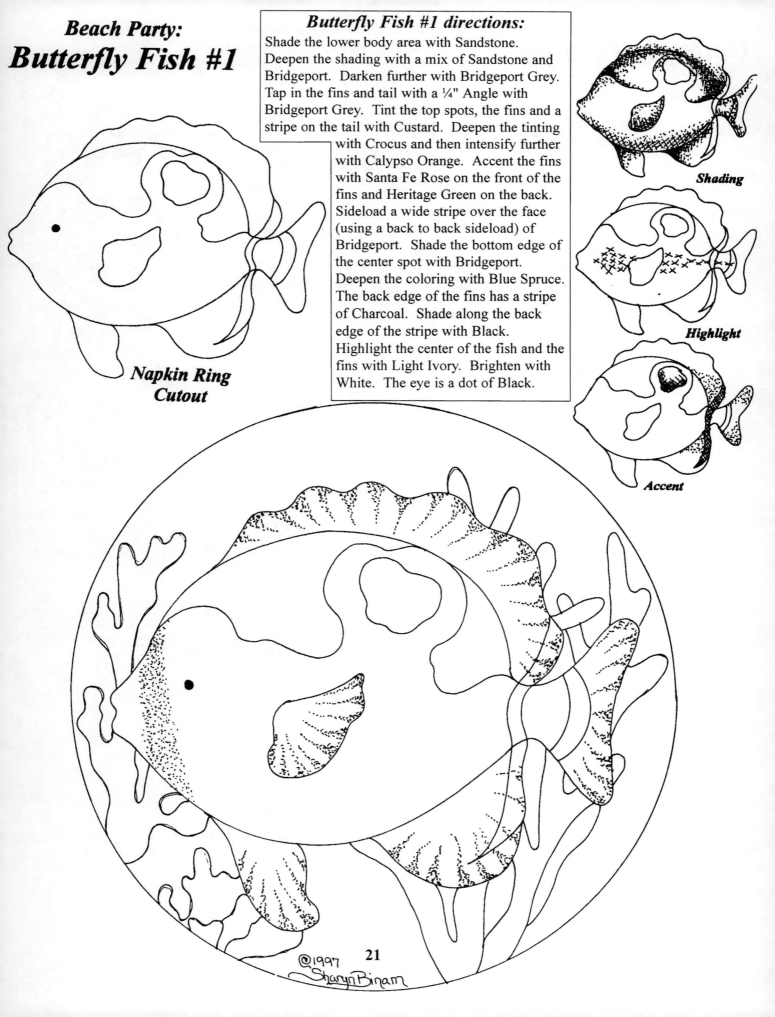

©1997
Sharyn Binam

21

Beach Party:
Butterfly Fish #2

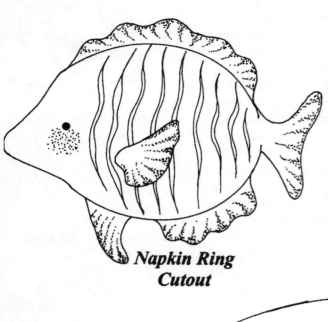

**Napkin Ring
Cutout**

Butterfly Fish #2 directions:
Tap in the fins with a ¼" Angle using Bridgeport Grey. Shade the body of the fish and the fins with Custard. Line the stripes with Mocha Brown. Deepen the shading on the body with Crocus. Darken further with Calypso Orange (or with Mocha Brown). Deepen the shading on the fins with Mocha Brown. Tint the cheek with a circular area of Bridgeport. Tint the fins with Heritage Green. The cheek spot may be intensified with Blue Spruce. Accent the fins next to the body with Santa Fe Rose. Highlight the center of the body and the fins with Light Ivory. Brighten the highlight with White. The eye is a dot of Black.

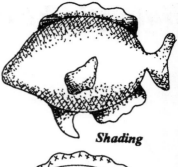

Shading

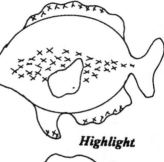

Highlight

Accent

©1997
Sharyn Binam

22

Beach Party:
Angel Fish

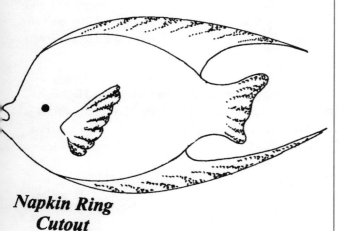

Napkin Ring Cutout

Queen Angel Fish:
Shade the body with Custard. Tap in the fins with a side-loaded ¼" Angle in Bridgeport Grey. Deepen the shading with Calypso Orange. Darken the shading using an accent of Heritage Green [ooo] as marked on the diagram. Apply tinting with Santa Fe Rose [;:::]. Accent further with Blue Spruce [////]. Highlight through the body with Light Ivory. Brighten the highlight further with White. Line the scales with Oasis Green.

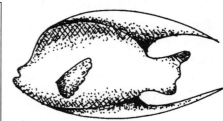

Shading

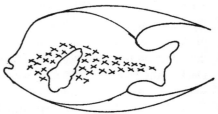

Highlight

Accent   [:::] Santa Fe Rose
[////] Blue Spruce
[oo] Heritage Green

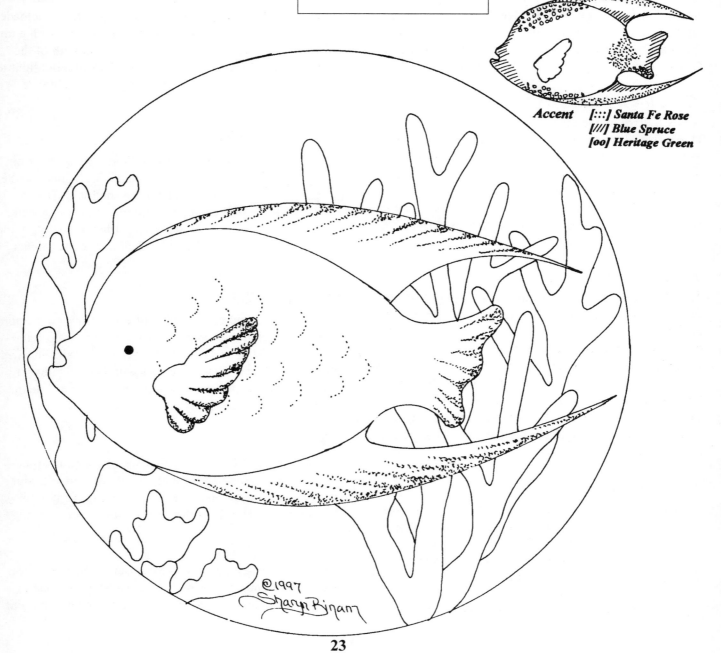

©1997
Sharyn Binam

23

The Tropical Reef:

The Paper Plate Holder, Utensil Holder and the Napkin, Salt and Pepper Holder from The Cutting Edge is a fun set to paint. I used green for my sea color but, a blue, teal or turquoise could be used. They could be enlarged for other surfaces. Remember, the larger they are, the more detail should be added...like scales for the fish. I hope you enjoy painting these as much as I had in designing them. Refer to the Tropical Fish instructions to paint the Moorish Idols and the Butterfly Fish along the reef. The background color is again Buttercream. The insides and the edges are Oasis Green.

The Rock Beauty Angel Fish:

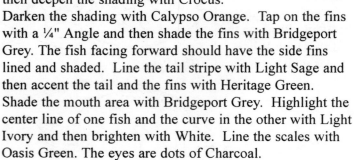

Apply a light wash of Custard on the pair of Rock Beauties. Shade with Custard and then deepen the shading with Crocus. Darken the shading with Calypso Orange. Tap on the fins with a ¼" Angle and then shade the fins with Bridgeport Grey. The fish facing forward should have the side fins lined and shaded. Line the tail stripe with Light Sage and then accent the tail and the fins with Heritage Green. Shade the mouth area with Bridgeport Grey. Highlight the center line of one fish and the curve in the other with Light Ivory and then brighten with White. Line the scales with Oasis Green. The eyes are dots of Charcoal.

The Clown Fish:

Apply a wash of Western Sunset Yellow over the little clown fish. Line the stripes with Light Ivory. Shade with Western Sunset along the outside edges of the fish between the stripes. Deepen the shading with Calypso Orange. Darken along the bottom edge including the lower fins with Santa Fe Rose. Highlight the center line of the fish with Light Ivory. Brighten the highlight with White. The eye is a dot of Charcoal.

The Anemone Fish:

The other little fish is a Anemone Fish. These two little fish could be exchanged if, an orange or a yellow fish was preferred. Apply a wash of Custard over the fish. Line the stripes with Light Ivory. Sideload a ¼" Angle and tap in the fins with Bridgeport. Shade the outside edges with Custard. Deepen the shading with Crocus. Darken the lower edge with Rosetta. Tint the mouth area with Bridgeport. Highlight the center line of the fish with Light Ivory. Brighten the highlight with White. The eye is a dot of Charcoal.

The Sea Horse:

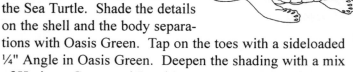

The little Sea Horses are attached to the sea grass and the sea fan with their tails. Apply a wash of Dunes Beige over the sea horses. Make a mix of Dunes and Bambi and line an 's' mark through the center of the body. Shade the outside edge with Bambi Brown. Tint the face and the fin with Lichen Grey. Deepen the shading

with Burnt Umber under the tail, fin and head. Highlight the center of the body with Light Ivory. If, more contrast is preferred, brighten the highlight with White. The eye is a dot of Charcoal.

The Sea Turtle:

Apply a wash of Light Sage over the Sea Turtle. Shade the details on the shell and the body separations with Oasis Green. Tap on the toes with a sideloaded ¼" Angle in Oasis Green. Deepen the shading with a mix of Heritage Green and Bambi Brown. Tint both of the lower edges of the shell with Bambi Brown. Highlight the shell, legs and head with Light Ivory. Eye is a dot of Charcoal.

The Crab:

Apply a wash of Dunes Beige over the little Crab. Shade the leg segments, the shell and under the shell with Dunes. Deepen the shading with Rosetta Pink. Darken further with Santa Fe Rose. Line the mouth with Bridgeport Grey. Highlight the shell and leg segments with Custard. The eyes are dots of Charcoal.

The Star Fish:

Shade the end and bottom edge of each arm with Western Sunset. Dots in the center of each arm are Territorial Beige made with an 18/0 Liner. Deepen the shading with Territorial Beige. Darken further with Burnt Umber if, more contrast is preferred. Highlight the center line of each arm with Light Ivory.

The Sand Dollar:

Dot the detail of the Sand Dollar with Raw Linen (or Lichen Grey) on an 18/0 Liner. Shade the outside edge with Ice Storm. Deepen the shading along the bottom with Lichen Grey. Highlight the center with White.

The Scallop Shell:

Line the shell segments with Raw Linen. Shade the top and bottom ends with Raw Linen. Deepen the shading with Sandstone. Darken the shading at the bottom point and the side fin with Lichen Grey. Apply two curved areas of Rosetta (using back to back floated color). Highlight the center of the shell with White.

The Sea Snail:

Line around the curved shell and then shade with Ice Storm to separate. Tap in detail lines around the outside edge with a mix of Ice Storm and Purple Smoke using an 18/0 Liner. Deepen the shading with the same mix of Ice Storm and Purple Smoke. Tint the inside of the shell with Dark Burnt Umber. Highlight the edge and down the center of the curves with White.

The Auger Shell:

Shade each segment at the outside edges with Raw Linen. Deepen the shading with Bambi Brown. Darken the lower edge with Dark Burnt Umber. Tint the inside of the shell with Rosetta Pink. Highlight the center line of the shell with White.

The Soft Coral:

Apply a wash of Village Green over the branches of the Soft Coral. Shade to separate the branches with a mix of Village Green and Heritage Green. Darken the shading on the back branches and the bottom edges with Heritage Green. Highlight the tips of the branches with Custard.

The Blue Coral:

Apply a wash of Light Sage over the branches of the coral. Shade the branches to separate with a mix of Light Sage and Heritage Green. Deepen the shading with a mix of Light Sage, Heritage Green and Purple Smoke. Or for a green color, darken the shading with just Heritage Green. Highlight the ends of the branches with Violet Ice or Custard.

The Sea Fan:

Set the ends of the Sea Fan with a tinting of Ice Storm. Line the branches with a wash of Light Sage with a #1 Liner. Shade to separate the branches with a mix of Light Sage and Oasis Green. I left the sea an very light but, it more contrast is preferred, deepen the shading with Oasis Green.

The Tube Sponge:

Apply a wash of Violet Ice over the sponge. Apply detail dots with Purple Smoke using a small liner. Shade to separate and inside the open tops with a mix of Violet Ice and Purple Smoke. Deepen the shading with Purple Smoke. Tint one side of each tube with Ice Storm. Highlight the center of each segment with White.

The Anemone:

Shade the ends of the arms with Oasis Green to set the intricate pattern. Apply a wash over the rest of the arms with a #1 or #2 Liner. Shade the bottom and center of the anemone with a mix of Oasis Green and Heritage Green. The ends may be shaded further with Heritage Green.

The Sea Grass:

Apply a wash of Village Green with a #2 Liner over the blades of long Sea Grass. Shade the grass to separate and define with a mix of Village Green and Green Sea. Deepen the shading with Green Sea. The tips or sides may be highlighted with Western Sunset Yellow.

The Rocks:

Sideload a ¼" Angle with a mix of Buttercream and Lichen Grey or with Bridgeport and tap in color randomly over the rocks. Shade the bottom edge with Lichen Grey. Deepen the shading with Dark Burnt Umber, again randomly tapping in the color along the bottom edge. Highlight with White or Light Ivory randomly to create more texture.

The Sand:

Thin Sandstone to the consistency of ink. Use a dip pen to make the sand grain dots as indicated on the detail drawing. Put a few gains over objects sitting in the sand. When the dots are completely dry, shade the sand area with Sandstone. Deepen the shading with Trail. Darken the shading further with Territorial Beige under the objects found in the sand.

The Sea:

Shade behind the sand and shells with Oasis Green. I shaded over the rocks and plants that are found at the edge of the sand when Oasis Green was applied a second time. The corners and edges of the wood piece are shaded with Oasis Green as well.

Beach Party:
Plate Holder

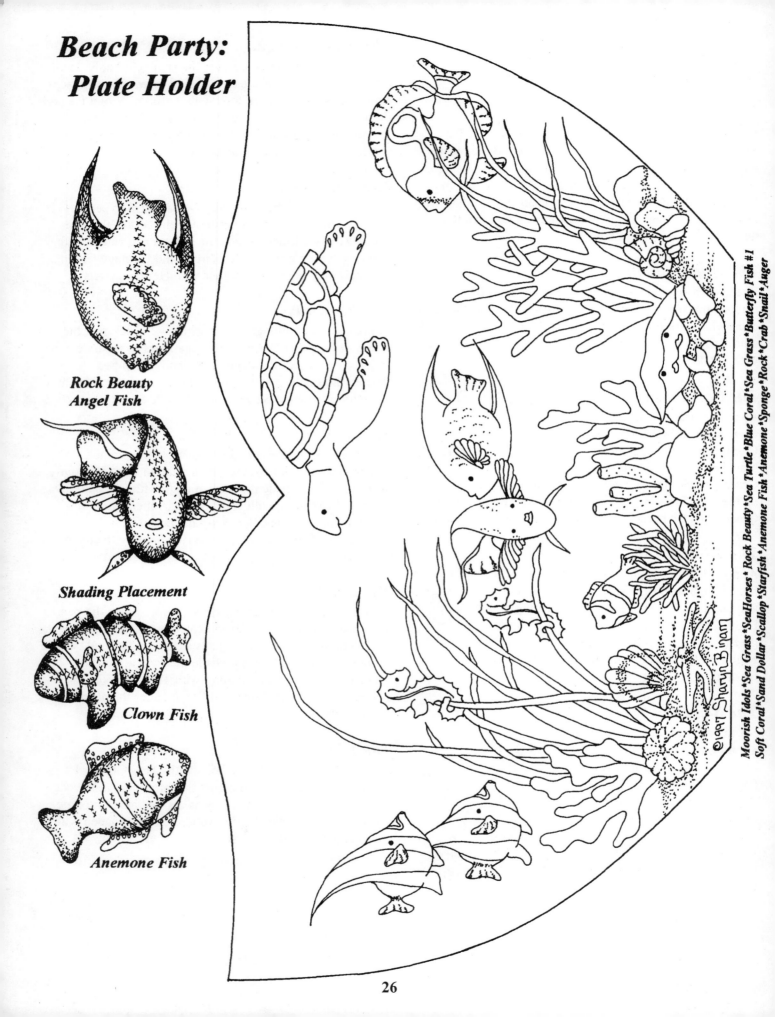

**Rock Beauty
Angel Fish**

Shading Placement

Clown Fish

Anemone Fish

Moorish Idols*Sea Grass*SeaHorses*Rock Beauty*Sea Turtle*Blue Coral*Sea Grass*Butterfly Fish #1
Soft Coral*Sand Dollar*Scallop*Starfish*Anemone Fish*Anemone*Sponge*Rock*Crab*Snail*Auger

©1997 Sharyn Binam

26

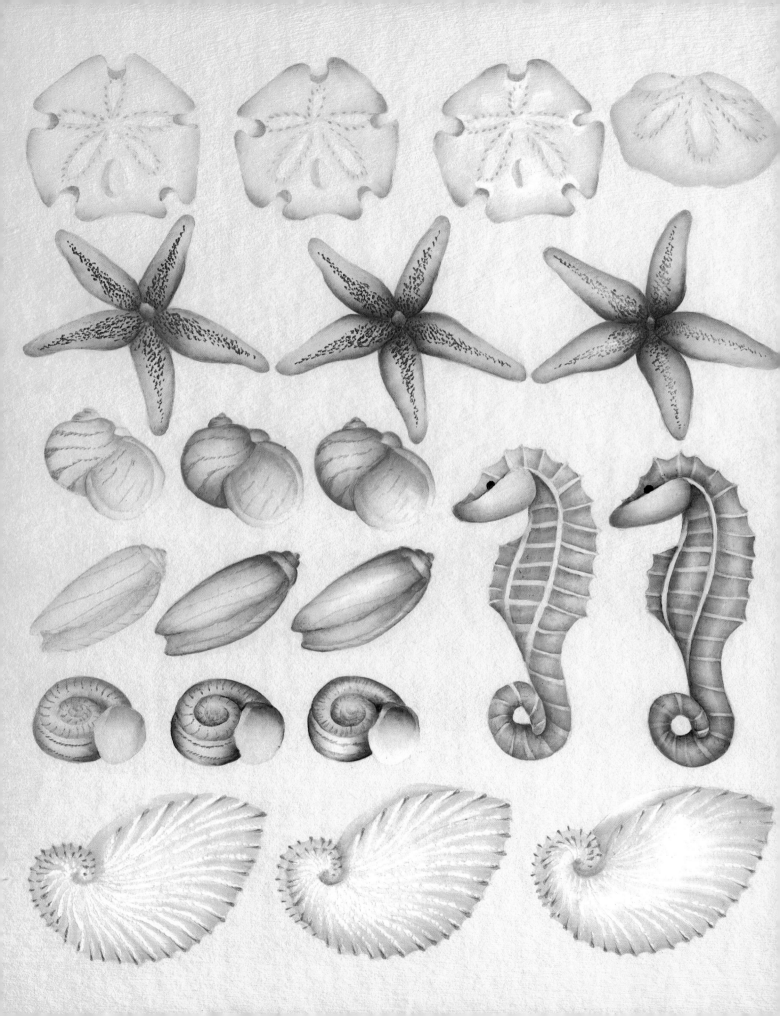

©1999 Sharyn Braun

Beach Party: Utensil Tote

Sea Horse Sea Fan Anemone Fish   Rock Beauty Sea Grass Sea Turtle Blue Coral
Auger   Rocks   Sponge Starfish   Rocks   Sand Dollar   Auger   Sea Snail

Sea Horses Sea Grass Clown Fish   Moorish Idols   Butterfly Fish #1
Sand Dollar Scallop Anemone Rocks Snail Auger Sponge Crab Soft Coral

Beach Party:
Napkin Holder

Star Fish

Shading Placement

Sea Horse

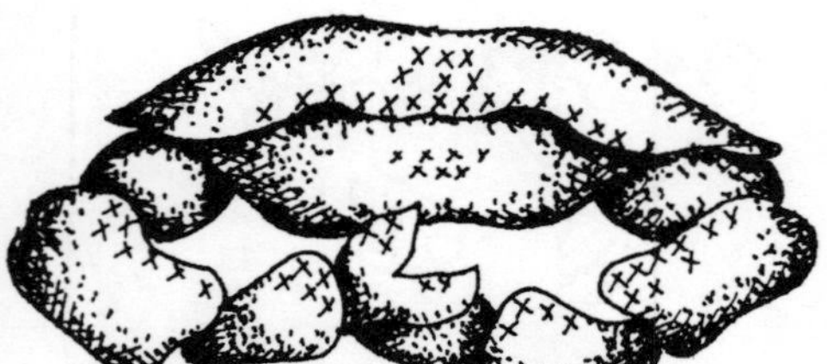

Crab

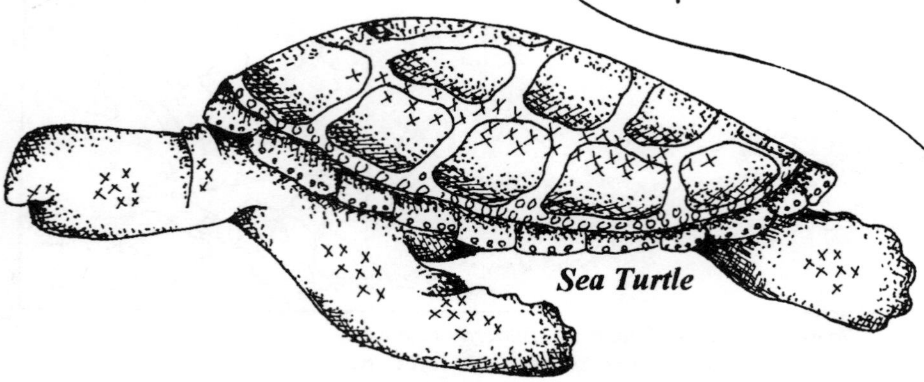

Sea Turtle

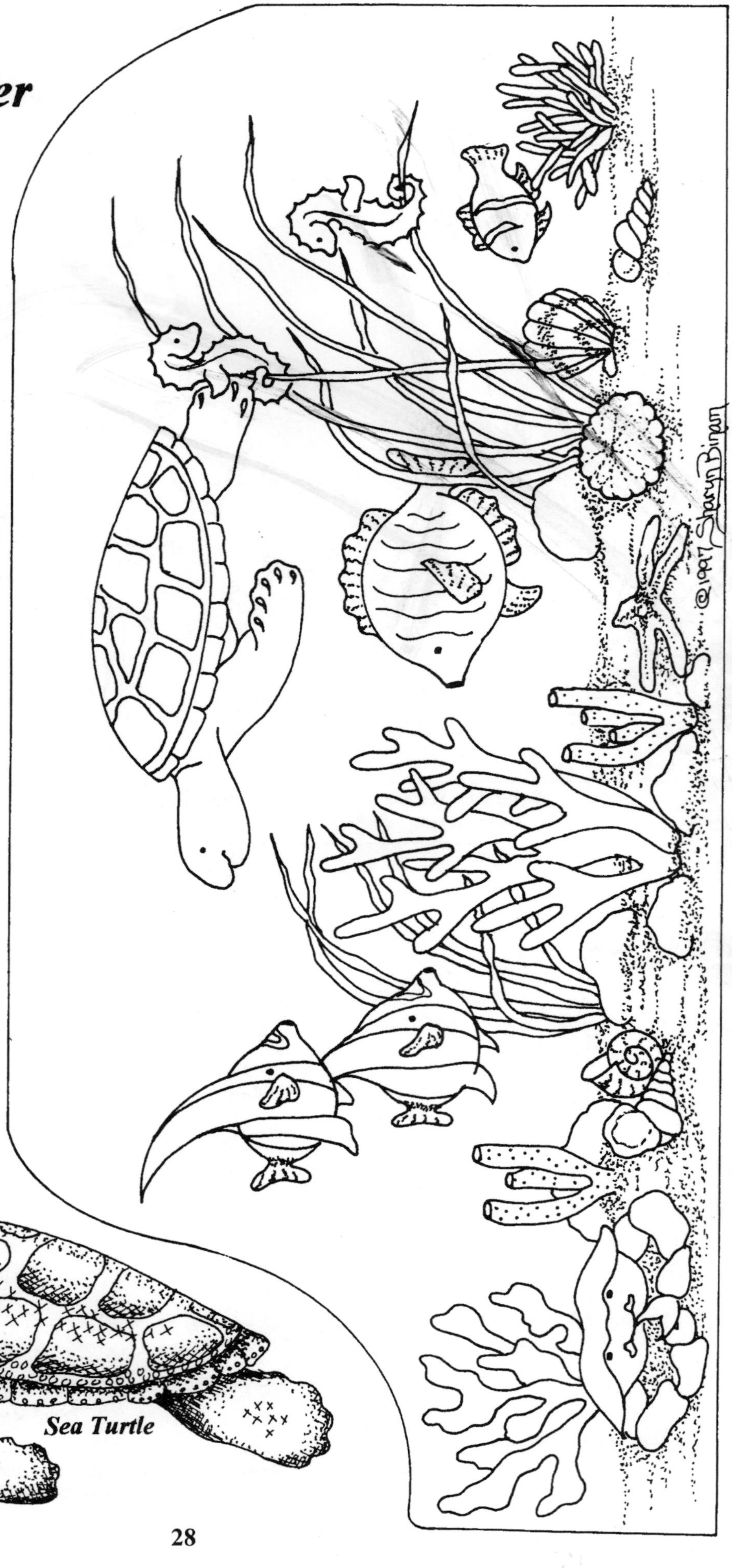

Soft Coral Sponge Moorish Idols Blue Coral Sea Turtle Butterfly Fish #2 Sea Grass Sea Horses
Crab *Auger *Sea Snail *Rocks *Sponge *Starfish *Sand Dollar *Scallop *Auger *Anemone Fish *Anemone

©1997 Susan Biram

28

Sea Shells Palette & Shading Chart

Delta Ceramcoat							
2025	Burnt Umber	2402	Sandstone	2447	Village Green	2496	Santa Fe Rose
2050	Mocha Brown	2419	Deep River Green	2454	Western Sunset Yellow	2505	White
2055	Autumn Brown	2424	Bambi Brown			2523	Buttercream
2118	Lichen Grey	2425	Territorial Beige	2466	Dunes Beige	2527	Dark Burnt Umber
2126	Medium Flesh	2430	Rosetta Pink	2470	Taupe	2546	Raw Linen
2401	Light Ivory	2435	Trail Tan	2472	Santa's Flesh	2548	Purple Smoke
		2445	Green Sea	2488	Mudstone	2555	Peachy Keen

AREA	SHADING	HIGHLIGHT	ACCENT	DETAILS
Arrowhead Sand Dollar	1: Raw Linen 2: Sandstone 3: Taupe	1: Light Ivory 2: White	Purple Smoke	Sandstone
Blue Starfish	1: Lichen Grey 2: Lichen + P.Smoke 3: Purple Smoke	1: Western Sunset 2: Light Ivory	Taupe	Lichen Grey + P. Smoke
Moon	1: Western Sunset 2: Bambi Brown 3: Mocha Brown	1: Light Ivory 2: White	1: Dunes 2: Santa Fe Rose	Lichen Grey
Olive	1: Western Sunset 2: Mocha Brown 3: Autumn Brown	1: Light Ivory 2: White	1: Dunes 2: Santa Fe Rose	Sunset + Mocha
Ram's Head Snail	1:Lichen Grey + Buttercream 2: Lichen Grey 3: Dark Umber	1: Light Ivory 2: White	1: Western Sunset 2: Mocha	Territorial Beige
Paper Nautilus	1: Raw Linen 2: Sandstone 3: Lichen Grey	1: Light Ivory 2: White	Taupe	White Lichen Grey
Scallop	1: Raw Linen 2: Sandstone 3: Lichen Grey	1: Light Ivory 2: White	1: Santa's Flesh 2: Rosetta Pink OR Taupe	
Sea Biscuit	1: Raw Linen 2: Sandstone 3: Lichen Grey	1: Light Ivory 2: White	Taupe	Sandstone
Sea Horse	1: Dunes Beige 2: Territorial Beige 3: Burnt Umber	1: Light Ivory 2: (White)		
Sugar Starfish	1: Western Sunset 2: Territorial Beige 3: Autumn Brown	1: Light Ivory 2: (White)	Santa Fe Rose OR Mocha Brown	Territorial Beige
Tellin	1: Raw Linen 2: Sandstone 3: Lichen Grey	1: Light Ivory 2: White	1: Santa's Flesh 2: Rosetta 3: Santa Fe Rose	
Tulip	1: Dunes Beige 2: Bambi Brown 3: Burnt Umber	1: Light Ivory 2: White	1: PeachyKeen 2: Med. Flesh 3: Santa Fe Rose	Lichen Grey
Top Shell	1: Dunes Beige 2: Taupe 3: Mudstone	1: Light Ivory 2: White	1: PeachyKeen 2: Med. Flesh 3: Santa Fe Rose	Lichen Grey
Urchin	1: Taupe 2: Taupe + P.Smoke 3: P.Smoke + Lichen	1: Western Sunset 2: Light Ivory	Lichen Grey Rosetta	Raw Linen
Whelk	1: Lichen Grey 2: Lichen + Umber 3: Dark Umber	1: Light Ivory 2: White	1: Santa's Flesh Trail 2: Rosetta	

Painting the Seashells

Arrowhead Sand Dollar:

Shade the outside edges between the indentations and around the five markings in the center with Raw Linen. Using a sideloaded ¼" Angle brush, tap in the details around the center markings with Sandstone. Shade both sides of the edges inside the indentations. Deepen all of the shadings with Sandstone. Darken the shading with Taupe. Taupe may be muted with Lichen Grey if preferred. Highlight the center of the indentations and the center of sand dollar with Light Ivory. Brighten the highlight areas with White.

Blue Starfish:

Shade around the center and along the outside of each arm with Lichen Grey. Add detail dots in the center of each arm with a mix of Lichen Grey and Purple Smoke. Deepen the shading with the mix of Lichen Grey and Purple Smoke. Darken the shading with Purple Smoke. Highlight the center of each arm with Western Sunset Yellow. Brighten the highlight with Light Ivory. Accent one side of each arm with Taupe.

Moon Shell:

Shade the outside of the shell with Western Sunset Yellow. Tap in the detail lines of Lichen Grey with a sideloaded ¼" Angle Brush. Deepen the shading with Bambi Brown. Darken the shading with Mocha Brown. Tint the inside of the shell with Dunes. Deepen the tinting with Santa Fe Rose. Highlight with Light Ivory. Brighten the highlight with White.

Olive Shell:

Shade the outside of the shell with Western Sunset Yellow. Tap in the detail lines with a mix of Western Sunset and Mocha Brown. Deepen the shading with Mocha Brown. Darken with Autumn Brown. Tint the inside of the shell with Dunes and deepen the tinting with Santa Fe Rose. Highlight with Light Ivory. Brighten the highlight with White.

Ram's Head Snail:

Shade around the curves of the shell with a mix of equal parts of Buttercream and Lichen Grey. Sideload a ¼" Angle Brush with Territorial Beige (or with Autumn Brown) and tap in the details. Deepen the shading with Lichen Grey. Darken further with Dark Burnt Umber (or with Burnt Umber for a warmer brown tone). Tint the inside of the shell with Western Sunset Yellow and then deepen the tinting with Mocha Brown. If a deeper color is preferred, darken the tint with Autumn Brown. Highlight the center of the curving shell with Light Ivory and then brighten with White.

Paper Nautilus:

Sideload a ¼" Angle Brush with White and tap along the dotted lines (as indicated on the detail drawings). Shade between the dotted lines from the edge to about ½" to ¾" into the shell. Use a tornado shaped stroke (back to back float) to form the indentations with Sandstone. Sideload a ¼" Angle Brush with Lichen Grey and tap the points (align with the white detail line). Shade around the shell with Raw Linen. Deepen the shading with Sandstone. Darken further with Lichen Grey. Tint the center curve and the top edge with Taupe. Highlight the center curve with Light Ivory. Brighten the highlight with White.

Scallop:

Line between the shell segments with Sandstone on a 10/0 Liner. Sideload a ¼" Angle Brush with Sandstone and tap in the details on the side fins. Shade the edges of the Scallop with Raw Linen. Deepen the shading with Sandstone. Darken the bottom with Lichen Grey. Tint the top and bottom areas with Santa's Flesh using a back to back float. Deepen the tinting with Rosetta Pink. Tint the sides with Taupe. Highlight the center of the shell with Light Ivory again using a back to back float. Brighten the highlight with White.

Sea Biscuit:

Shade around the Sea Biscuit and the center markings with Raw Linen. Sideload a ¼" Angle Brush with Sandstone (or Lichen Grey) and tap in the details around the center markings. Deepen the shading with Sandstone. Darken the shading with Lichen Grey or with a mix of Lichen Grey and Taupe. Highlight the center of each marking and the curve of the Sea Biscuit with Light Ivory. Brighten the highlight with White.

Sea Horse:

Shade inside each segment with Dunes Beige. First, shade along the vertical lines then, along the horizontal lines. Shade the lower edge of the head and behind the jaw. Deepen the shading with Territorial Beige along the vertical lines. Deepen the shading with Burnt Umber. A very light shading of Burnt Umber or Territorial Beige may also be applied to the entire outside edge. Highlight the center of each half of the body with Light Ivory using a back to back float. If more contrast is preferred, brighten the highlight with White.

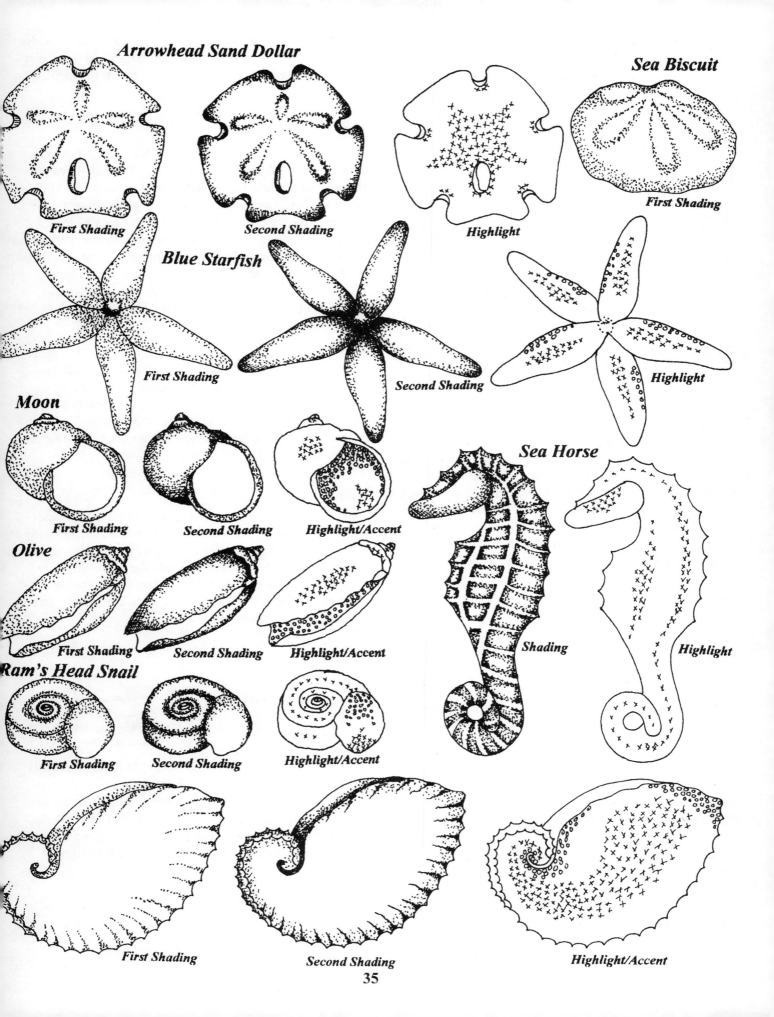

Arrowhead Sand Dollar

First Shading

Second Shading

Highlight

Sea Biscuit

First Shading

Blue Starfish

First Shading

Second Shading

Highlight

Moon

First Shading

Second Shading

Highlight/Accent

Sea Horse

Olive

First Shading

Second Shading

Highlight/Accent

Shading

Highlight

Ram's Head Snail

First Shading

Second Shading

Highlight/Accent

First Shading

Second Shading

Highlight/Accent

35

Sugar Starfish:

Place detail dots along the center of each arm in circular shapes with Territorial Beige or with Autumn Brown. Shade the Starfish with Western Sunset Yellow. Deepen the shading with Territorial Beige. Darken further with Autumn Brown. Tint the top edge of each arm with Santa Fe Rose (or with Mocha Brown). Highlight the center of each arm with Light Ivory. Brighten further with White for more contrast.

Tellin:

Tint the stripes with Santa's Flesh first along one side of each stripe and then the other. Shade the outside of the shell with Raw Linen. Deepen the shading with Sandstone. Darken further with Lichen Grey. Deepen the tinting with Rosetta along the front and down the sides. Darken further with Santa Fe Rose if more color is preferred. Highlight the center of the shell with Light Ivory using a back to back float. Brighten the highlight further with White.

Tulip:

Shade with Dunes Beige. Tap in the detail lines with Lichen Grey using a ¼" Angle Brush. Deepen the shading with Bambi Brown. Darken further with Dark Burnt Umber or with Burnt Umber for a warmer brown. Tint the inside of the shell with Peachy Keen. Deepen the tinting with Medium Flesh. For more color, darken the tint with Santa Fe Rose. Highlight the shell with Light Ivory. Brighten with White.

Top Shell:

Shade the shell with Dunes. Tap in the detail lines with Lichen Grey using a sideloaded ¼" Angle Brush. Or use Lichen Grey dots made with a liner or dip pen. Add a few dots in Taupe, Peachy Keen and Raw Linen for variety. Deepen the shading with Taupe. Darken with Mudstone. Tint the inside of the shell with Peachy Keen. Deepen the tint with Medium Flesh. For more color, darken the tint with Santa Fe Rose.

Urchin:

Shade along each segment line and inside the opening with Taupe using a tornado shaped stroke (back to back float). Deepen the shading with a mix of Taupe and Purple Smoke along the segments, inside the opening and along the bottom edge. Dip a stylus in Raw Linen and begin in the center of the urchin shell making descending dots towards the top and then towards the bottom along each segment line. Darken the shading with Purple Smoke muted slightly with a touch of Lichen Grey. Tint the top

outside edge with Rosetta Pink. Lichen Grey can be added along the center top as a cool accent. Highlight the center curve with Western Sunset Yellow. Brighten the highlight with Light Ivory.

Whelk:

Shade the edges of the shell with Lichen Grey. Tap in the details with Trail Tan sideloaded on a ¼" Angle Brush. Deepen the shading with a mix of Lichen Grey and Dark Burnt Umber. Darken the shading with Dark Burnt Umber. Tint the inside of the shell with Santa's Flesh. Deepen the tinting with Rosetta. For more color, darken the tinting with Santa Fe Rose. Highlight the outside of the shell with Western Sunset Yellow and then brighten with Light Ivory. Highlight the inside along the curve with Light Ivory and then brighten with White.

Sand:

Using a dip pen (Crow Quill Pen) and thinned Trail Tan (or for a lighter use sand color Sandstone), make dots as indicated on the detail drawings. Wipe the pen on a paper towel when the dots become larger: about every 2 or 3 minutes. When the dots are dry, shade with Trail. Deepen the shading with Territorial Beige.

Grass:

Shade the outside edges of the grass blades with Village Green. Deepen the shading with Green Sea soften slightly with a touch of Village Green. Deepen the shading with Deep River Green. Accent/highlight the grass with a mix of Green Sea and Territorial Beige. For more detail to the grass blades, tap in random veining lines that are parallel to the edges with Green Sea.

Basket:

Using a sideloaded ¼" Angle Brush tap in the detail lines with a mix of equal parts of Buttercream and Lichen Grey. Shade between the reeds with that same mixture.  Deepen the shading with Lichen Grey. If more contrast is referred, darken the shading with Mudstone or with a mix of Lichen Grey and Dark Burnt Umber. Highlight the center of the reeds with Light Ivory. Shade behind the shells and under the rim with Lichen Grey. This shading may be deepened with the mix of Lichen Grey and Dark Burnt Umber.

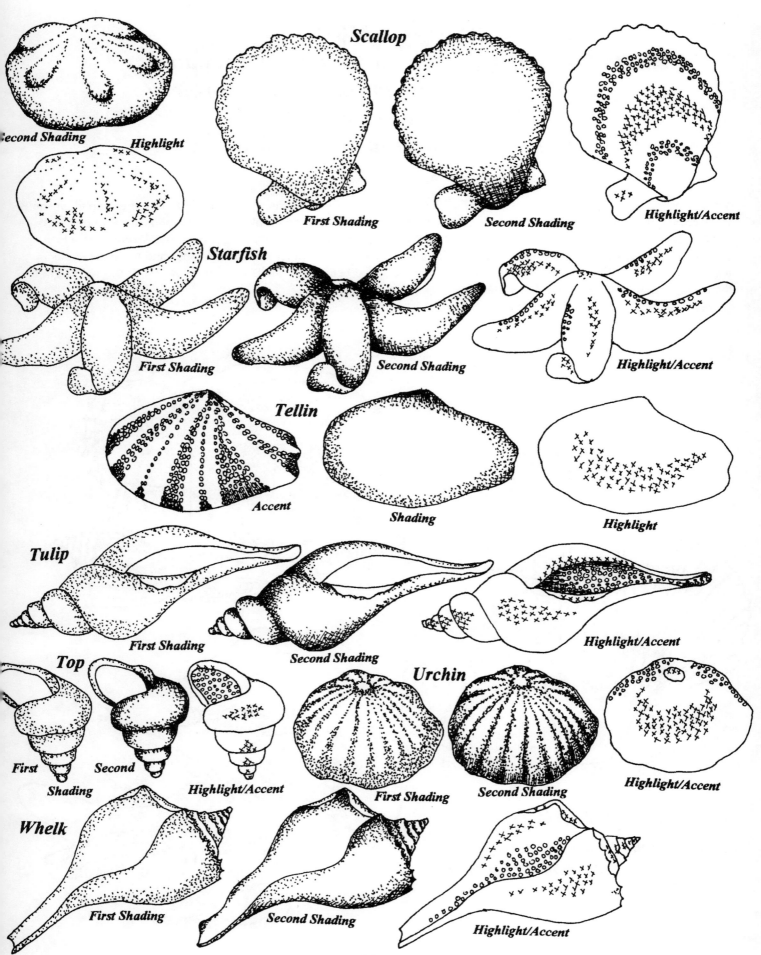

Scallop

Second Shading Highlight

First Shading Second Shading Highlight/Accent

Starfish

First Shading Second Shading Highlight/Accent

Tellin

Accent Shading Highlight

Tulip

First Shading Second Shading Highlight/Accent

Top

First Shading Second Highlight/Accent

Urchin

First Shading Second Shading Highlight/Accent

Whelk

First Shading Second Shading Highlight/Accent

37

Seashell Projects
The following pages contain the directions, patterns and shading placements for the seashell projects found on color pages 32, inside back cover and back cover.

The 9 seashell projects are combinations of the 15 seashells shown in the center paint-out. Painting the individual shells is described in the preceding section. Along with the center paint-out, shading placement diagrams are also provided. Make a copy (you have permission for your personal use only) of the Shell Painting Chart for quick reference while painting. The shells can be combined to make additional designs to suit other surfaces. I used sand to tie the shells together throughout the designs. Beach grass can also be added behind the shells for added interest or to give height to the design when fitting it to another surface.

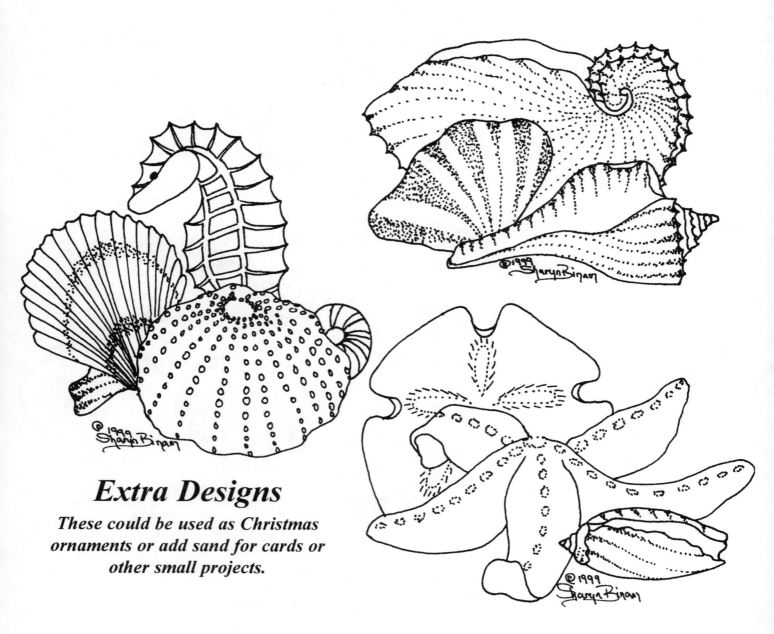

Extra Designs
These could be used as Christmas ornaments or add sand for cards or other small projects.

Bucket of Shells

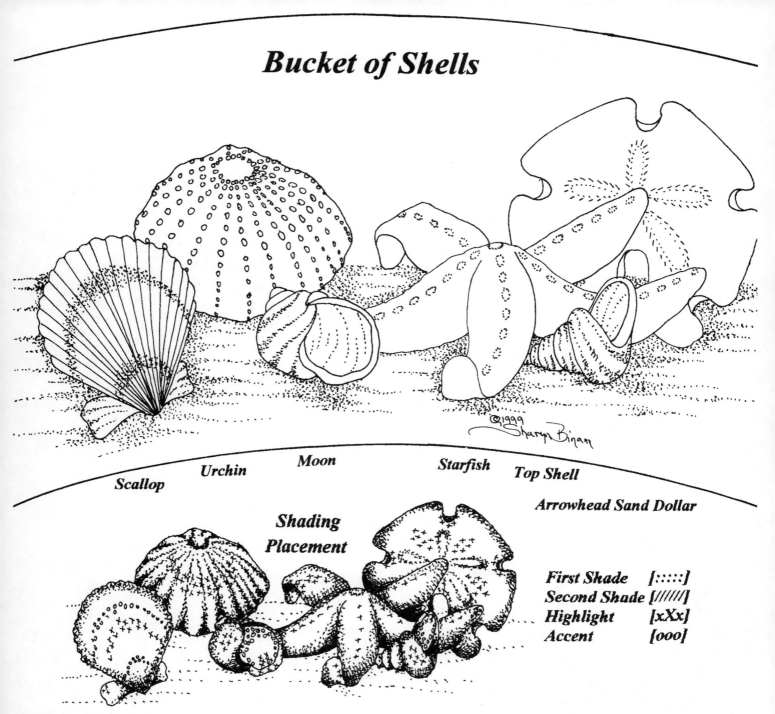

©1999 Sharyn Binam

Scallop　　Urchin　　Moon　　Starfish　　Top Shell

Arrowhead Sand Dollar

Shading Placement

First Shade	*[:::::]*
Second Shade	*[//////]*
Highlight	*[xXx]*
Accent	*[ooo]*

Bucket of Shells:

This wooden Bucket from The Cutting Edge is basecoated with Buttercream with Raw Linen inside. The handle and the bottom have cording glued around. Basecoat with Buttercream (or Raw Linen) or leave the cording natural. Shade around the top edge to soften the transition between the inside and outside.

I used the bucket as a holder for a shell topiary. Topiary forms are available in a variety of shapes and sizes. I chose a small round form that fit into the bucket. The dowel and the top of the base were covered with cording. I used a low melt glue gun to attach the shells to the top. The shells were overlapped to cover the green styrofoam as well as bunches of the "berries" used in the other accessory pieces. Loops of cording were used to make a bow. I used both gathered and purchased shells in the topiary and around the base. A flower pot could be used to hold a larger topiary. Enlarge the design to fit.

This design features a Scallop, Urchin, Moon, Starfish, Top Shell and Sand Dollar. Refer to the instructions for painting each shell or use the Shell Painting Chart for quick reference. The sand may be applied with Trail or with Sandstone thinned to the consistency of ink to work in a dip pen. Shade the Trail sand with Trail and then with Territorial Beige; shade the Sandstone sand with Sandstone and then Trail or Lichen Grey.

39

Shell Collection

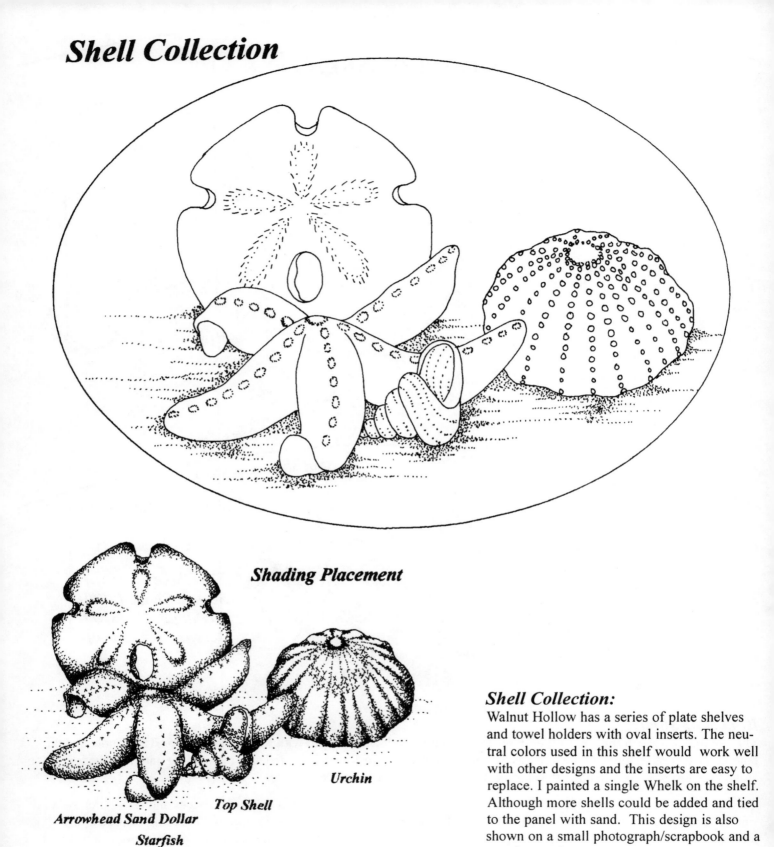

Shading Placement

Arrowhead Sand Dollar

Starfish

Top Shell

Urchin

Shell Collection:
Walnut Hollow has a series of plate shelves and towel holders with oval inserts. The neutral colors used in this shelf would work well with other designs and the inserts are easy to replace. I painted a single Whelk on the shelf. Although more shells could be added and tied to the panel with sand. This design is also shown on a small photograph/scrapbook and a greeting card.

Shell Collection features a Sand Dollar, Urchin, Top Shell and Starfish. Refer to the instructions for the individual shells or the Shell Painting Chart for quick reference.

The sand grains are applied with a dip pen in Trail or Sandstone. Shading over the Trail sand is Trail and then Territorial Beige; for Sandstone use Sandstone and then Trail or Lichen Grey.

Basket of Shells:

The rectangular box from The Artist's Club was basecoated with Buttercream. I did not trim the edges on the sample. I glued the cording to the sides of the base (which was about an entire package) with Delta's Quik 'n Tacky. The cording can be painted with Raw Linen or Buttercream. I left the cording natural and applied a coat of Matte Exterior/Interior Varnish liberally over the cording for protection.

The shells in this design are Olive, Blue Starfish, Arrowhead Sand Dollar, Top Shell, Sea Horse, Scallop, Whelk, Ram's Head Snail, Paper Nautilus, Tellin, Tulip, Urchin, Moon and Sea Biscuit. Refer to the instructions for each shell or use the Shell Painting Chart for quick reference.

The Basket is shaded with a mix of Buttercream and Lichen Grey. Sideload a ¼" Angle Shader with Lichen Grey and tap in the detail lines using the detail diagram as a guide. Deepen the shading on the reeds with Lichen Grey. Highlight the center of each reed with Light Ivory. Shade behind the shells, under the top rim and edges with Lichen Grey. If more contrast is preferred, deepen the shading with a mix of Lichen Grey and Dark Burnt Umber.

The sand grains are applied using a dip pen and paint thinned to the consistency of ink. Used either Trail or Sandstone for the grains. Shade the sand with Trail and then Territorial Beige over the Trail grains; shade with Sandstone and then Trail or Lichen Grey over the Sandstone grains.

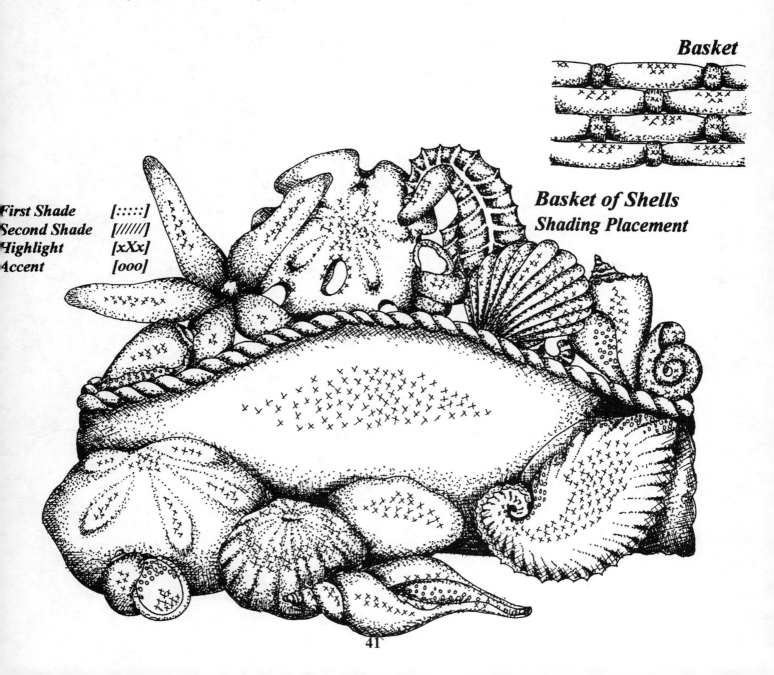

Basket

First Shade   [::::::]
Second Shade [//////]
Highlight   [xXx]
Accent   [ooo]

Basket of Shells
Shading Placement

Basket of Shells

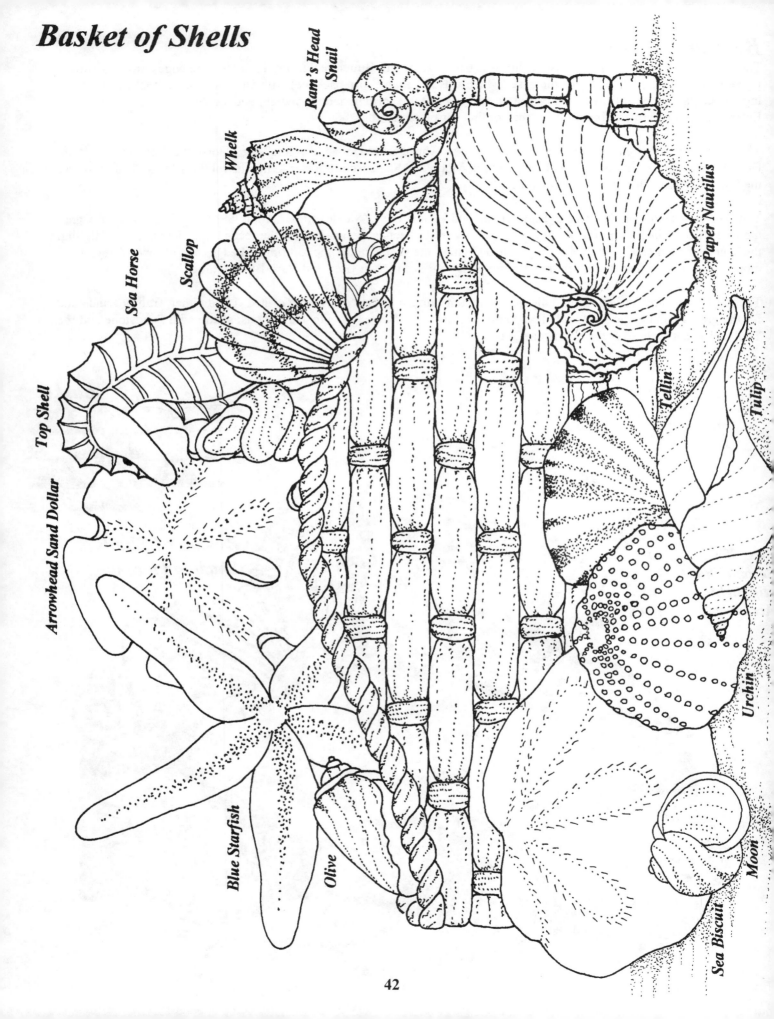

Ram's Head Snail

Whelk

Sea Horse

Scallop

Top Shell

Arrowhead Sand Dollar

Blue Starfish

Olive

Paper Nautilus

Tellin

Tulip

Urchin

Moon

Sea Biscuit

Beach Mementos:

The cork memo board from The Artist's Club has a top panel for painting and a bottom panel covered with cork. I had 6 shells cut from ¼" (or use 3/16") birch plywood for the thumb tacks. Drill the back of each shell with a 3/8" Forstner bit about 1/8" deep. Use Bond 527 to glue metal thumbtack and wood together. Paint the shells using the individual shell instructions. Once the panel and frame are painted and varnished, use plastic window screen holders (hardware store: replace the packaged screws with shorter screws). The panels are flush with the back of the frame so, mirror holders and screen door spline cannot be used to hold the panels. The edges of the frame were trimmed with Raw Linen.

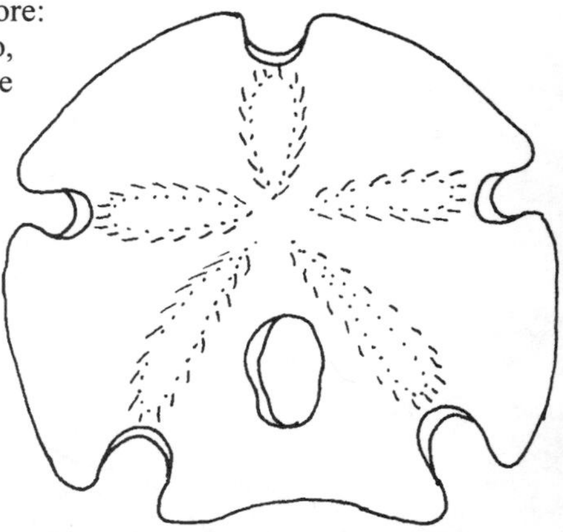

The shells in this design are Arrowhead Sand Dollar, Paper Nautilus, Urchin, Olive, Ram's Head Snail, Tulip and Scallop. Refer to the instructions for the individual shells or the Shell Painting Chart for quick reference.

The Beach Grass is shaded along the edges with Village Green. Deepen the shading with a mix of equal parts of Village Green and Green Sea. Darken the shading with Deep River Green. To coordinate the colors in the sand with the grass,

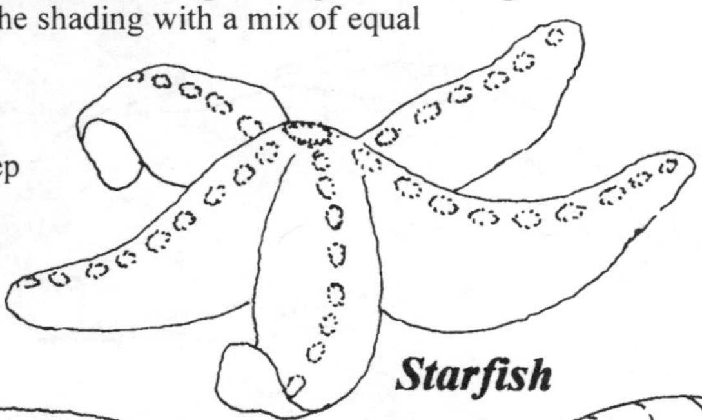

Arrowhead Sand Dollar

Top Shell

Starfish

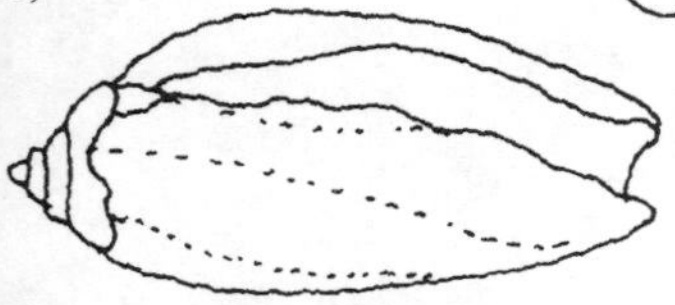

Olive

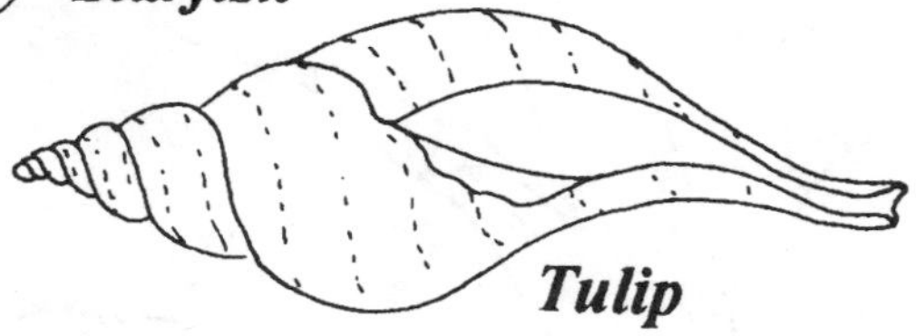

Tulip

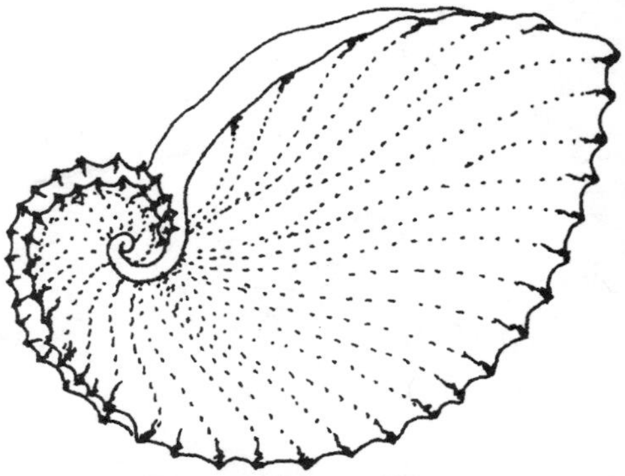

Paper Nautilus

highlight/tint the edges with a mix of Green Sea and Territorial Beige. If more detail is preferred, side-load a ¼" Angle Shader with Green Sea and tap in vein lines parallel to the edges.

The sand grains are either Trail or Sandstone applied with the dip pen. Shade over the Trail with Trail and then Territorial Beige and over the Sandstone grains with Sandstone and then Trail or Lichen Grey.

Arrowhead Sand Dollar

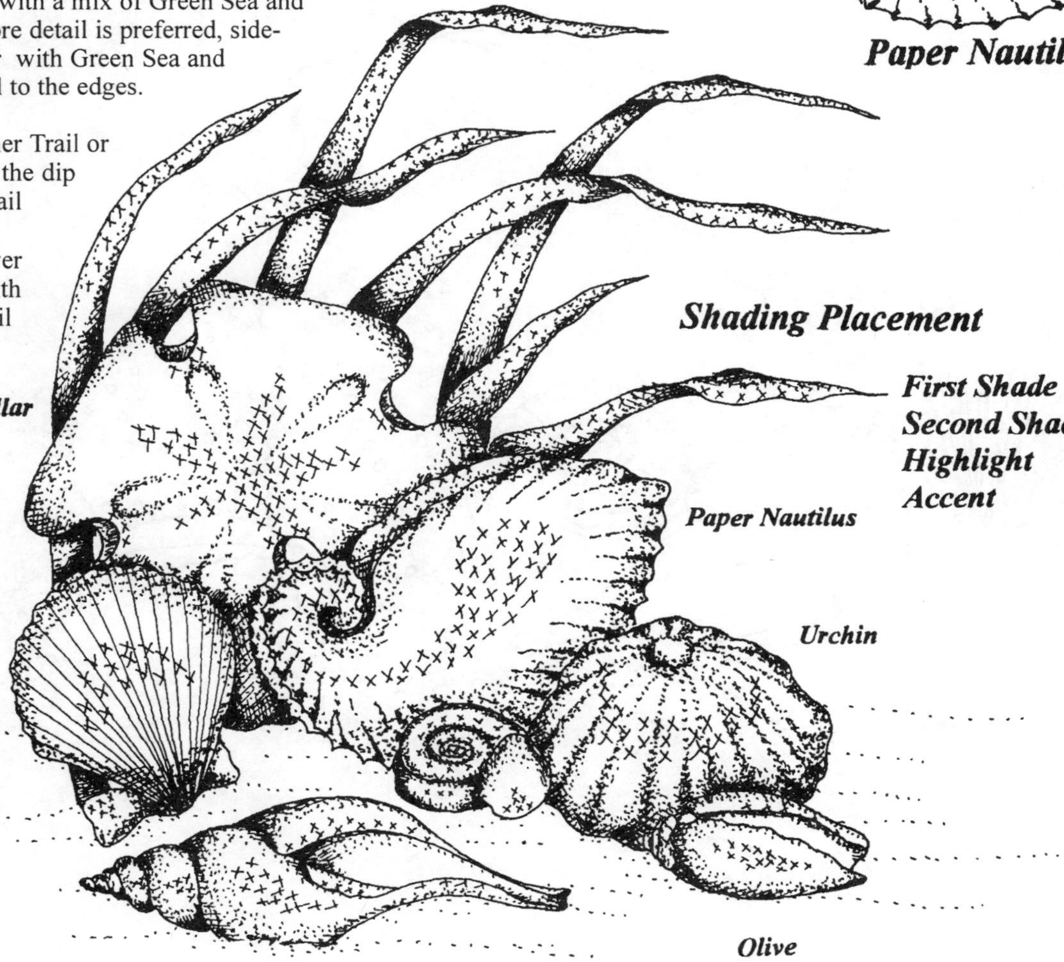

Shading Placement

First Shade	[:::::]
Second Shade	[//////]
Highlight	[xXx]
Accent	[ooo]

Paper Nautilus

Urchin

Scallop

Tulip   **Ram's Head Snail**   43

Olive

Beach Mementos

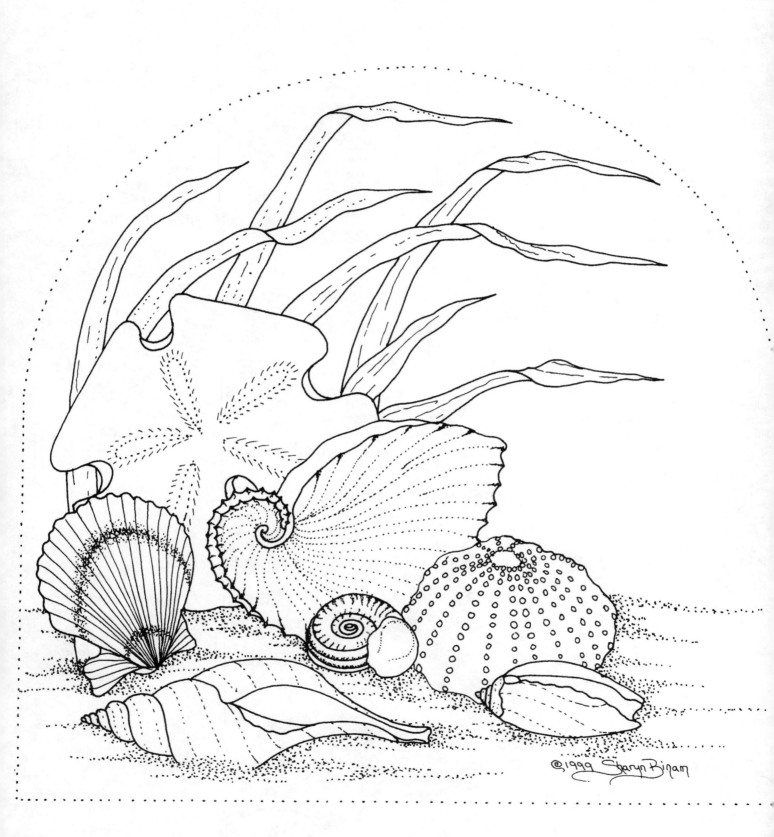

©1999 Sharyn Binam

Beach Treasures:

This cabinet from Wayne's Woodenware has 4 drawers (for recipes in the kitchen or cosmetics, etc. in the bath - or almost anything!) and a lidded top section. Their cabinets come in 2 drawer and 4 drawer styles with and without the lidded section. Trim the edges and the insides of the drawers with Raw Linen. The drawer designs can be centered or placed to the outside of the cabinet. I also used the drawer designs on greeting cards. They are, of course, also suitable for other small projects. The corners of the drawers and the front panel can be shaded with Raw Linen.

Most of the 15 shells are used in the project. Refer to the instructions for the individual shells or the Shell Painting Chart for quick reference while painting.

Beach Treasures

Shading Placement

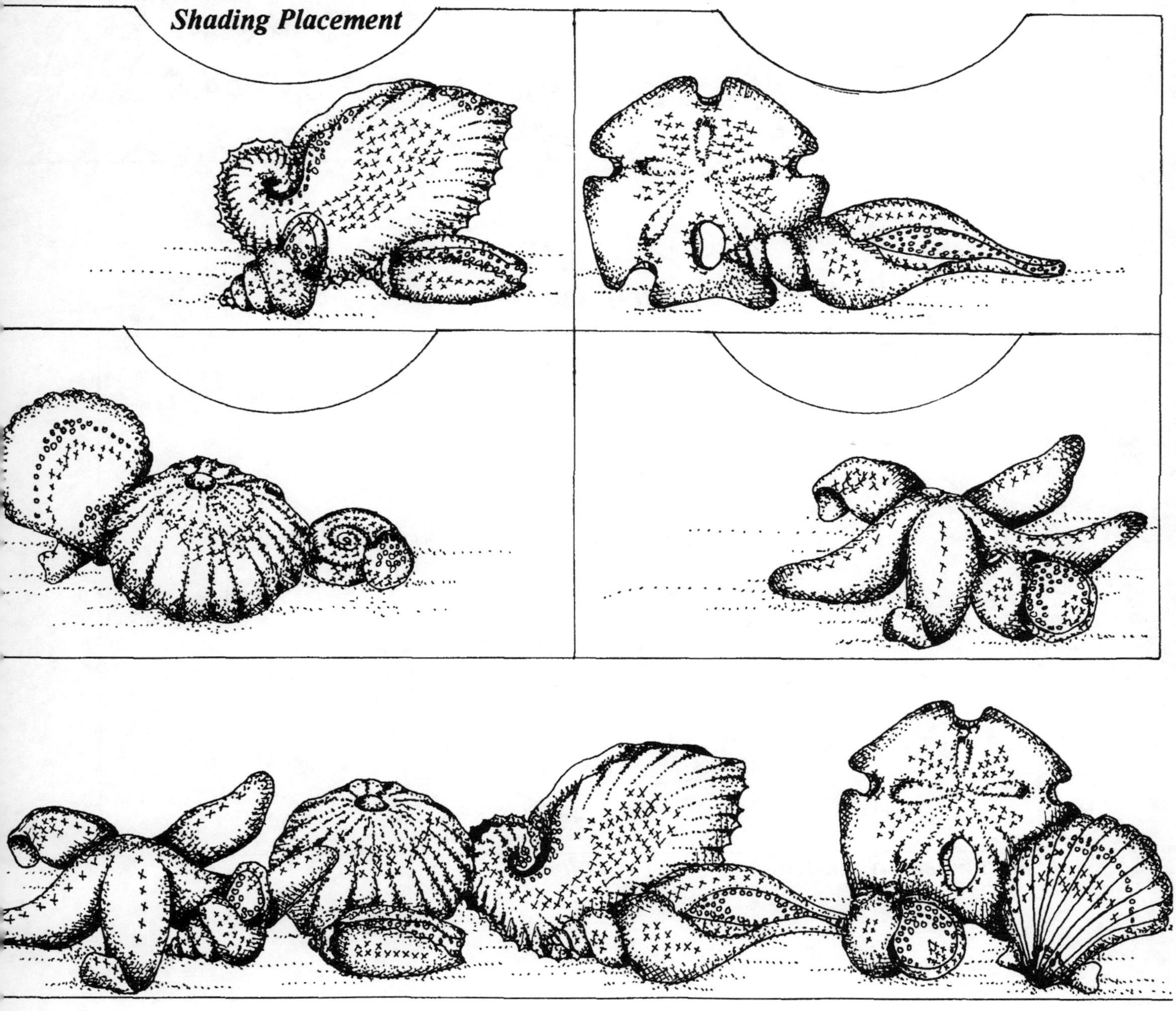

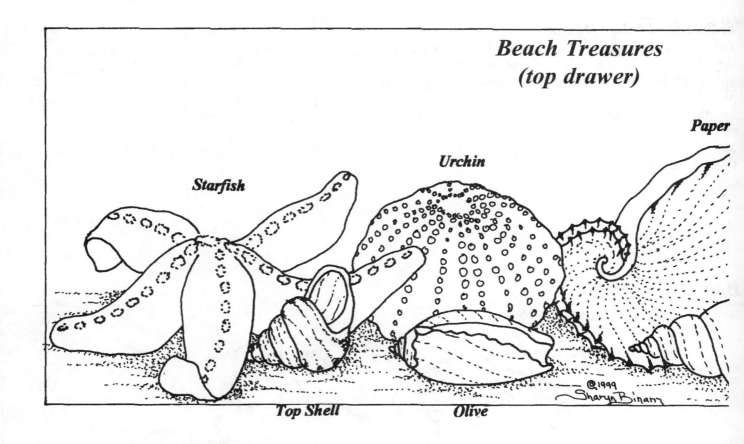

Beach Treasures
(top drawer)

Paper

Urchin

Starfish

Top Shell   Olive

Beach Treasures
(left middle drawer)

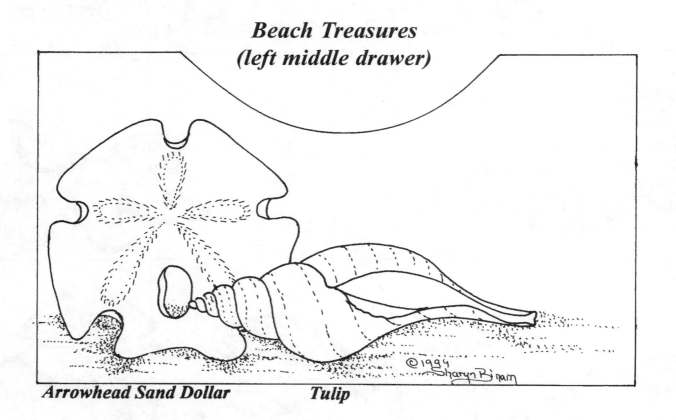

Arrowhead Sand Dollar   **Tulip**

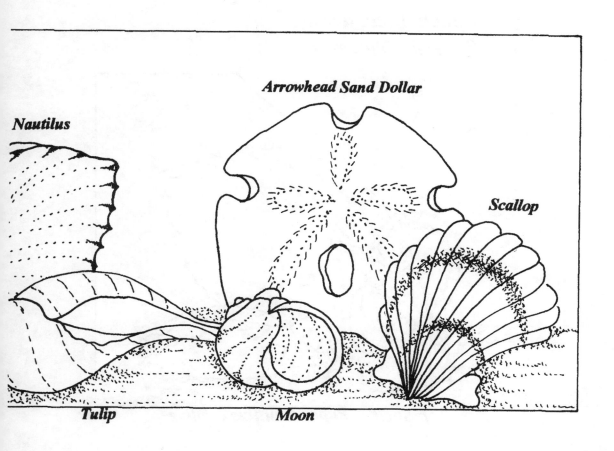

Nautilus

Arrowhead Sand Dollar

Scallop

Tulip   **Moon**

Beach Treasures
(right middle drawer)

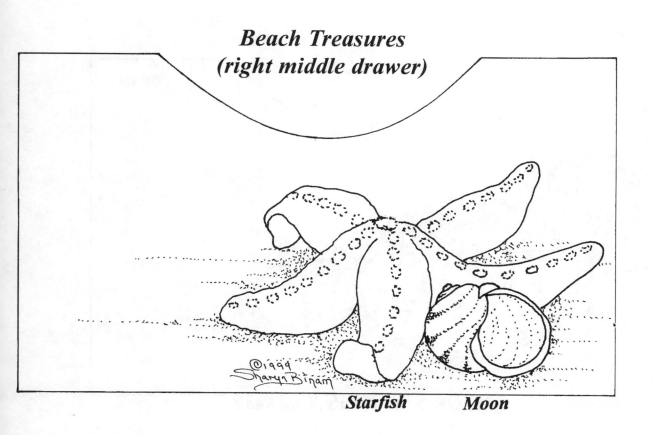

©1999
Sharyn Binam

Starfish   **Moon**

Beach Treasures
(bottom drawers)

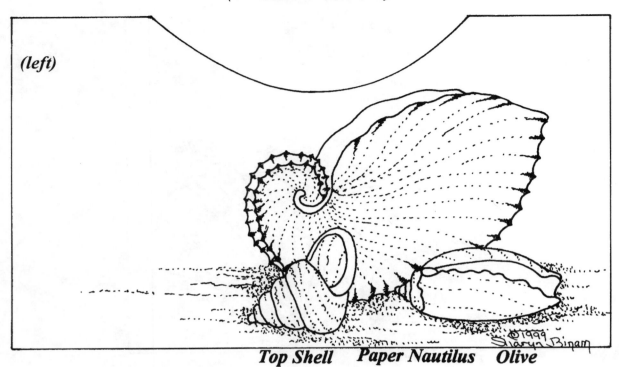

(left)

Top Shell   **Paper Nautilus**   **Olive**

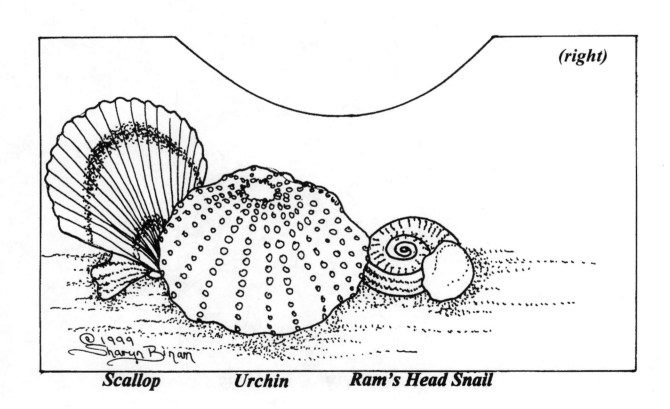

(right)

Scallop   **Urchin**   **Ram's Head Snail**

Shell Clock:

The round clock from Walnut Hollow has the new paint-able hands which can be sprayed or based with a cosmetic sponge in acrylic paint. The hands should be varnished before assembly. The edges are Raw Linen. Shade behind the shells and around the outside edge with Raw Linen. The shading can be deepened with Sandstone.

Again most of the shells appear in this design. Refer to the instructions for the individual shells or to the Shell Painting Chart for quick reference while painting.

Shell Clock
Shading Placement

First Shade	*[:::::]*
Second Shade	*[///////]*
Highlight	*[xXx]*
Accent	*[ooo]*

Shell Clock

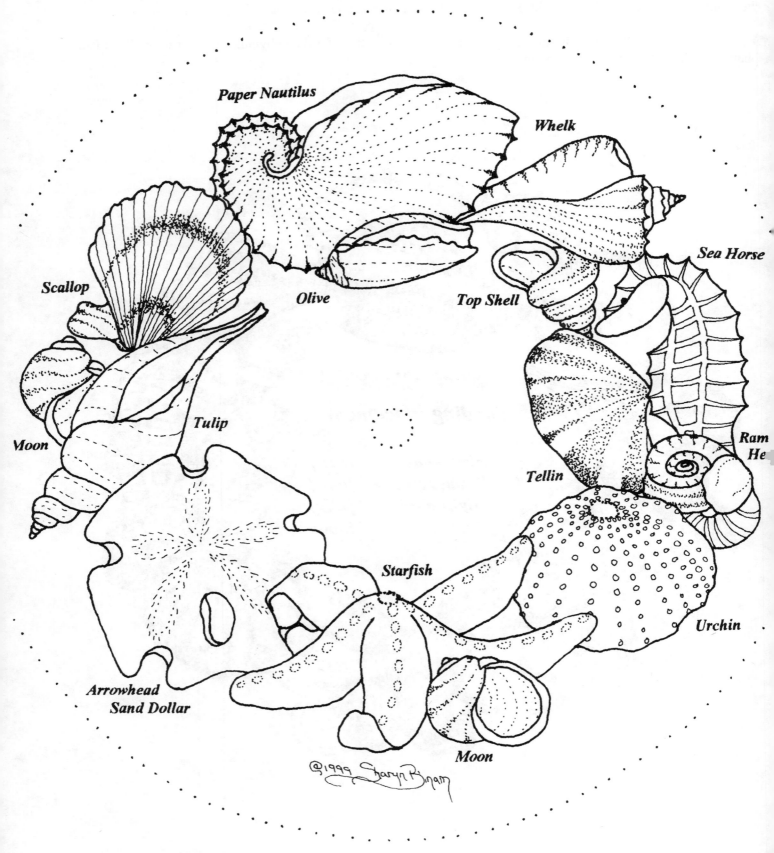

Paper Nautilus

Whelk

Sea Horse

Scallop

Olive

Top Shell

Ram He

Moon

Tulip

Tellin

Starfish

Urchin

Arrowhead
Sand Dollar

Moon

©1999 Sharyn Bingam

50

Shell Wreath
Shading Placement

First Shade	**[:::::]**
Second Shade	**[//////]**
Highlight	**[xXx]**
Accent	**[ooo]**

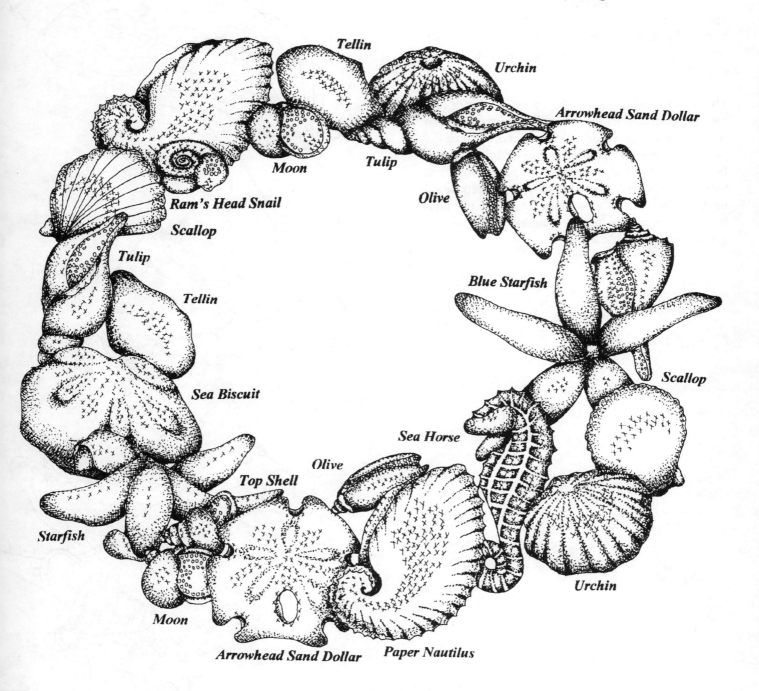

Tellin

Urchin

Arrowhead Sand Dollar

Moon

Tulip

Olive

Ram's Head Snail

Scallop

Blue Starfish

Tulip

Tellin

Scallop

Sea Biscuit

Sea Horse

Olive

Top Shell

Starfish

Urchin

Moon

Arrowhead Sand Dollar

Paper Nautilus

Shell Wreath:

The new collapsible tables from J.B Wood Products are a great idea! There are several different table shapes available. The table can be glued together permanently or the interlocking legs and top are stable if the table is temporary, to be shipped as a gift or stored flat. Mark the back of the table top and align the legs. Glue the braces to the back before painting using Delta Wood-Wiz glue. Basecoat the top and legs with Buttercream. The edges of the top and the legs are Raw Linen. Shade around and behind the shells and around the outside edge with Raw Linen. Deepen the shading with Sandstone if more color is preferred.

This design features all of the 15 shells. Refer to the painting instructions for the individual shells or the Shell Painting Chart for a quick reference while painting. I used a turntable to make painting the fairly heavy table top easier. Lifting and moving the table can be inconvenient while trying to reposition for each shell. Use the turntable (a plastic turntable from Rubbermaid is inexpensive and works well) to quickly turn the table top.

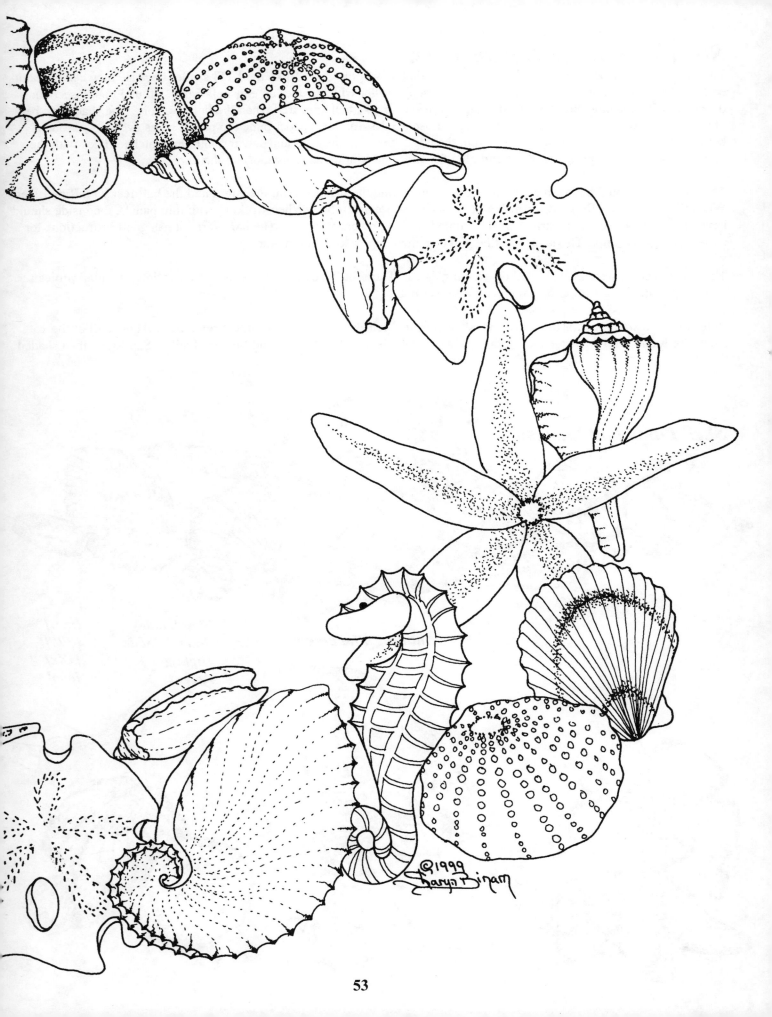

©1999
Sharyn Dinan

Shell Lamp and Lampshade:

The Lamp base is from Walnut Hollow and the shade kit is from KITI. I like the KITI shades because they can be painted flat. The shade should be basecoated using a sponge roller which leaves an eggshell finish. I found that basecoating the shade with a sponge brush or brush tended to leave streaks that appeared when the light was on. The shade can be glued together when the painting is completed. I use a 3/16" (or 1/8") paper punch to punch holes every ½" through both ends of the shade about ¼" to 3/8" from the edge. Overlap the ends and sew through the matched holes with the cording used on other projects. Knot and glue the ends and trim the cording close to the knot.

The lamp base should be taken apart and painted (including the inside). Trim the edges and the ball feet with Raw Linen. When the designs are finished, varnish all the pieces before assembly. When working with thin panels, the inside should have the same basecoat and varnish as the painted side to prevent warping. The hardware kit has good instructions for easily wiring the lamp. The lamp must be wired as the lamp base is assembled.

The panel designs were also painted on greeting cards. These little designs can be used on a variety of small projects. The lampshade design could be painted on a flower pot.

Refer to the instructions for the individual shells or the Shell Painting Chart for quick reference. Almost all of the 15 shells are found on the lampshade. Again the sand is applied with a dip pen and thinned Trail or Sandstone then shaded.

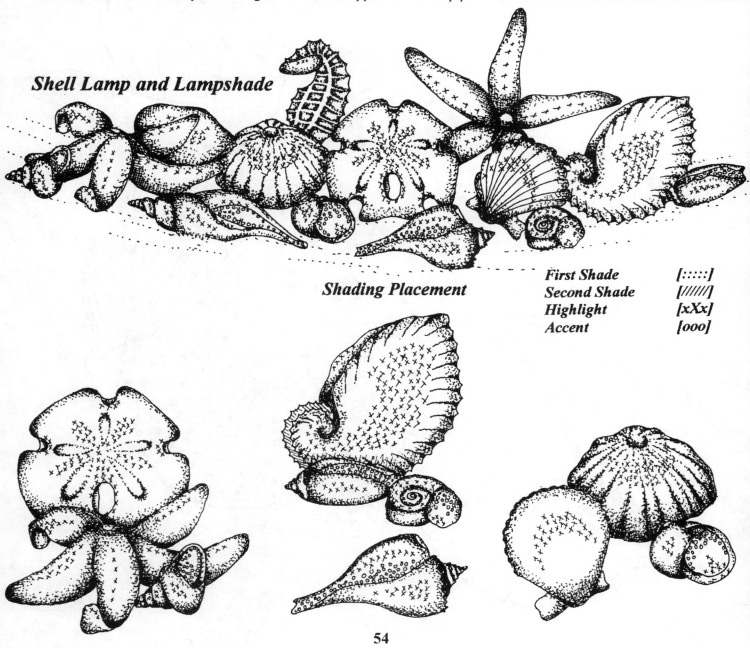

Shell Lamp and Lampshade

Shading Placement

First Shade	*[::::::]*
Second Shade	*[//////]*
Highlight	*[xXx]*
Accent	*[ooo]*

Shell Lamp

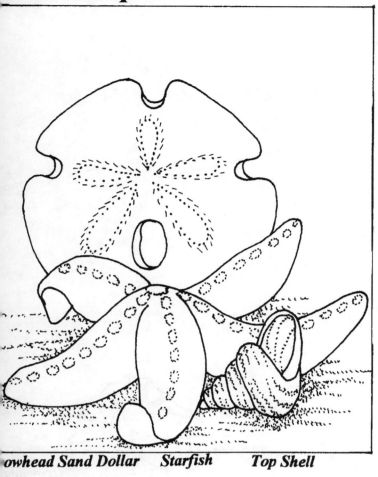

owhead Sand Dollar   Starfish   Top Shell

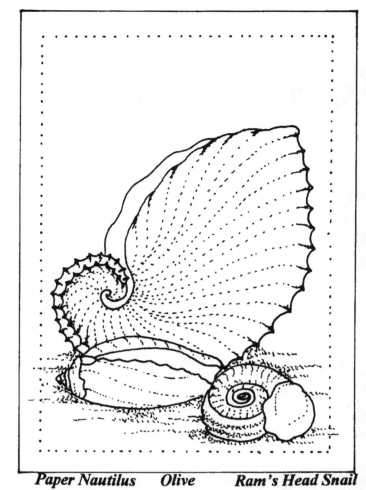

Paper Nautilus   Olive   Ram's Head Snail

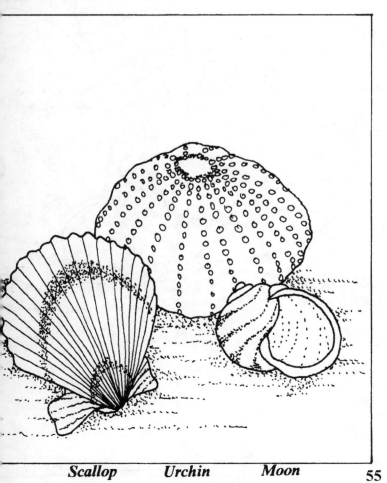

Scallop   Urchin   Moon

55

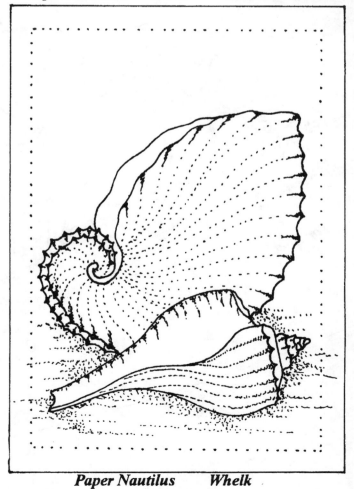

Paper Nautilus   Whelk

Shell Lampshade

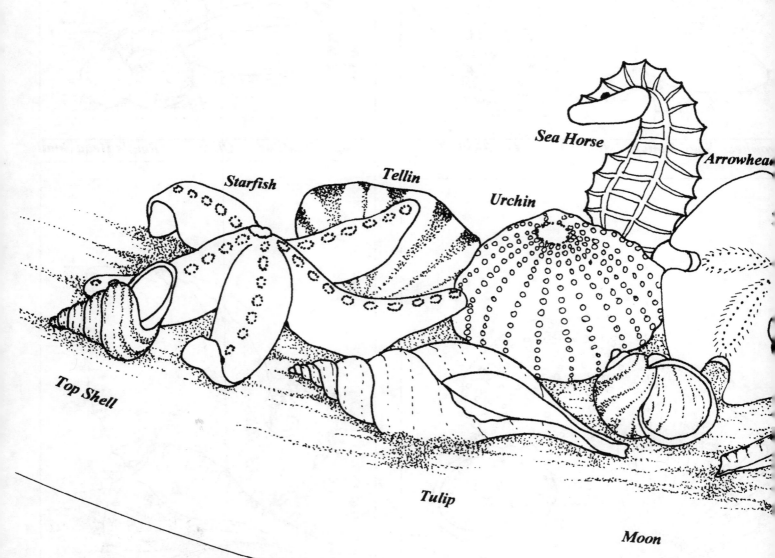

Sea Horse

Arrowhea[d]

Starfish

Tellin

Urchin

Top Shell

Tulip

Moon

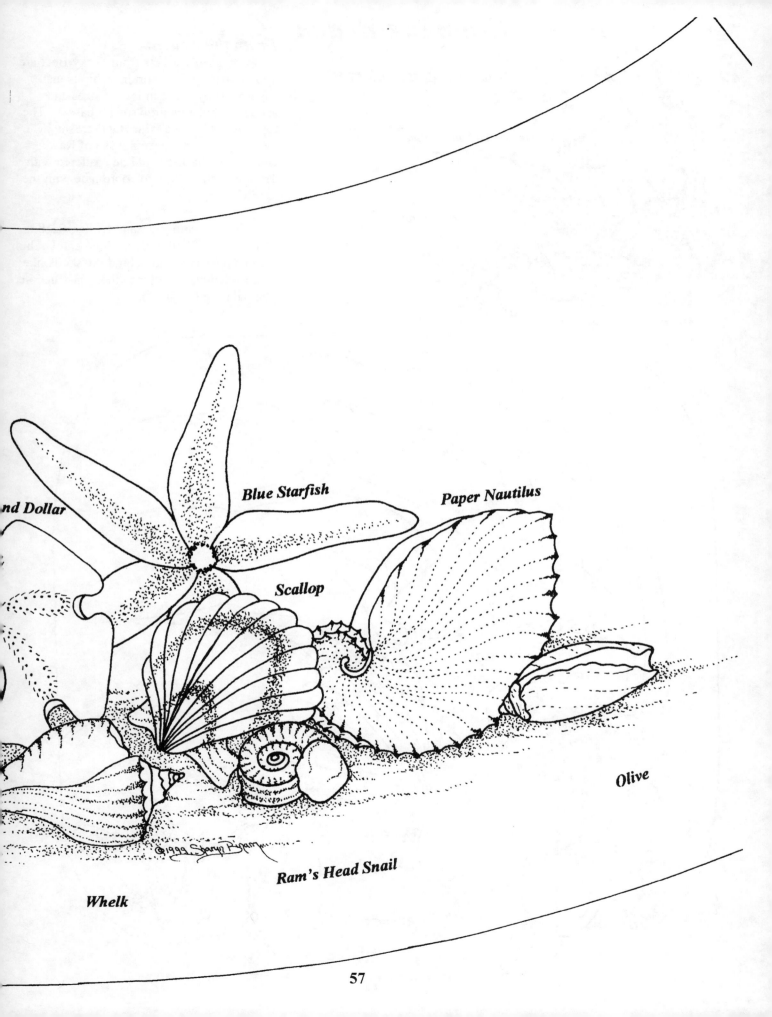

nd Dollar

Blue Starfish

Paper Nautilus

Scallop

Olive

©1999 Sharyn Byram

Ram's Head Snail

Whelk

From the Beach

Shading Placement

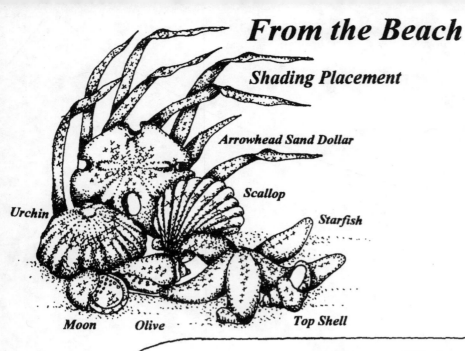

Arrowhead Sand Dollar

Scallop

Starfish

Urchin

Moon   **Olive**   **Top Shell**

From the Beach:
The wonderful baskets from Pesky Bear are a joy to paint. The workmanship is just superb. They come in lots of sizes and shapes: I love this little square basket. The top was basecoated with Buttercream. The basket and handle have a wash of Raw Linen. The basket could be spattered with Trail or Lichen Gray to coordinate with the sand.

This design features a Sand Dollar, Scallop, Starfish, Top Shell, Olive, Moon and Urchin. Beach Grass is found behind the shells like Beach Mementos (refer to those instructions will painting the grass).

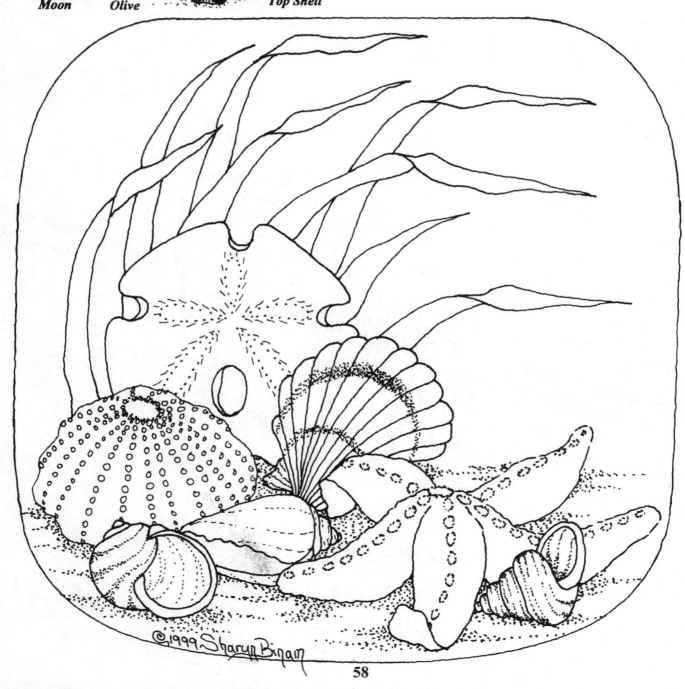

©1999 Sharyn Binam